What People Are Saying About Lorraine and Robert...

"Lorraine and Robert helped me change my focus so much we have restructured our business so I don't have to be there anymore; I'm there sometimes but that is by my choice. My team are far more productive and so am I. Some of the organizational strategies they have helped me put in place have allowed me to concentrate on our larger clients. So I'm out and about dealing with them. With their help we have produced increased sales and profitability. Robert and Lorraine have gained my gratitude for what we have been able to achieve and I am quite happy to recommend them to you without reservation."

Gary Quin; QLD

"We will always be grateful for the expert knowledge and guidance that Rob and Lorraine extended throughout the time that they worked with us. Our business was in a growth phase that we were struggling to manage. From the beginning Lorraine and Rob strategically worked with us to develop systems and procedures that kept our business moving forward. They held us accountable and gave us the tools we needed to develop ourselves and change our mindset for success – this wasn't always easy, however knowing that Lorraine and Rob had our backs and cared about our success, made it possible. Rob and Lorraine have an extensive knowledge of what makes a business successful. They coached us in the area of sales, marketing, human resources, management, financial control and strategic planning. Working with Lorraine and Rob ultimately created growth and success which we never believed that we were capable of both professionally and personally.

Warning: Do not work with Lorraine and Rob unless you want massive results."

Joanna Neale – Anderson Plumbing

“I have known Robert and Lorraine personally and professionally for almost 20 years. Collectively they possess a high level of knowledge and expertise across a wide range of industries and business sectors.

Their achievement focus through strategic, yet practical planning has been an invaluable resource in implementing new marketing programs, recruitment, IT, processes and systems, amongst many others, for my business that is in an aggressive growth phase.

Their ‘down to earth’ nature is at times perplexing as their focus on driving results for my business sees them being upfront at times, as their success is a direct correlation of the success that I enjoy.”

Kim Kershaw – Kim Kershaw Finance Solutions

“I just want to say a big fantastic amazing thank you to Lorraine and Rob for helping us with our business and our marketing. Lorraine and Rob are both amazing people. They have got great skills and having two people together is like having two coaches for the price of one! We have increased our profits and turnover by 32% in the last 12 months and we are very happy and now we have even bigger goals for the rest of this year and the next 12 months.

If you are thinking about having a Business Coach definitely, definitely, consider Lorraine and Rob, I couldn’t recommend them more highly. Enjoy business, it’s a great ride.”

Michelle Patterson – Balloonaversal Entertainments

"I have been working with Lorraine and Rob as my business coaches for several months now with the primary business objective in engaging them to focus on business growth.

Lorraine and Rob's expertise in business is immediately recognisable. They have been able to offer advice from a practiced business background which has been invaluable in redirecting my business focus.

They have unlocked areas of the business which I hadn't considered. Seeing opportunities, which were not in my view previously, translating into new revenue avenues.

Lorraine and Rob are always available and respond immediately to SOS calls. To have the support behind me and someone to discuss business direction is invaluable.

They are genuinely engaged in the growth of my business."

Kelly Royle – Kelly Royle Landscape Architecture

"Lorraine and Robert are as determined as a kid learning to ride a bike. They have excelled in every aspect of the projects we have been completing. We have to thank both Lorraine and Robert for their commitment to us and our company. They are extremely passionate life and business coaches and they motivate you to get the job done. I can honestly say that without their support we wouldn't have completed anywhere near as much as we have.

A massive thank you to both Lorraine and Robert. "

Cameron Resource – Recoveries & Recycle

"I have to give both Lorraine and Robert a massive thank you. They have been there for me from the beginning and genuinely care about my success. Their wealth of knowledge and expertise across such a wide range of businesses has helped my business to have amazing results and a massive increase in sales. There is so much to learn about having a successful business and they have guided me all the way with changing my focus and applying different strategies. They keep me motivated and their support and encouragement has kept me going when things get overwhelming.

They are down to earth, positive people who are committed to my success. I am so grateful for the opportunity to work with Lorraine and Robert and would strongly recommend working with them."

Lisa Vannucci – Diamante Events

"It was great to speak with you today. Thank you for your brilliant coaching and support."

Aldwyn Altuney – AA Xpose Media

"The book, Moment of Impact, is written really clearly and I found it easy to understand, even though I have absolutely no background in business at all. It certainly highlights the whole range of areas that most new or prospective small business owners need to consider before and during the process of buying and running a business.

I personally appreciated the external references to Stephen Covey, personality quadrants and such because I think they demonstrate that you have utilised knowledge from other well-known sources as opposed to just making stuff up yourself; they add to the credibility of what you are saying.

Finally, I think it is a great marketing tool for your business coaching! It is personal, relevant and logical."

Adrienne Dudley
Assistant Principal, Ivanhoe East Primary School

Moment of IMPACT

GLOBAL
PUBLISHING
GROUP

Global Publishing Group
Australia • New Zealand • Singapore • America • London

Moment of IMPACT

How We Went From Losing Millions to Making Millions & How You Can Too...

A TRUE STORY WITH LESSONS NO-ONE TELLS!

LORRAINE BROOKS
& ROB DUNCAN

Foreword by Alex Mandossian
Author, Master Trainer & International Marketing Expert

DISCLAIMER

All the information, techniques, skills and concepts contained within this publication are of the nature of general comment only and are not in any way recommended as individual advice. The intent is to offer a variety of information to provide a wider range of choices now and in the future, recognising that we all have widely diverse circumstances and viewpoints. Should any reader choose to make use of the information contained herein, this is their decision, and the contributors (and their companies), authors and publishers do not assume any responsibilities whatsoever under any condition or circumstances. It is recommended that the reader obtain their own independent advice.

This work depicts actual events in the life of the authors as truthfully as recollection permits and/or can be verified by research. Occasionally, dialogue consistent with the character or nature of the person speaking has been supplemented. All persons within are actual individuals; there are no composite characters. The names of individuals have been changed to respect their privacy.

First Edition 2017

Some names and identifying details have been changed to protect the privacy of individuals.

National Library of Australia

Cataloguing-in-Publication entry:

Creator: Brooks, Lorraine, author.

Title: Moment of Impact : How We Went From Losing Millions to Making Millions & How You Can Too / Lorraine Brooks & Rob Duncan.

ISBN: 9781925288650 (paperback)

Subjects: Success in business.
Wealth.
Industrial management.
Business consultants.
Achievement motivation.

Other Creators/Contributors: Duncan, Rob, author.

Published by Global Publishing Group
PO Box 517 Mt Evelyn, Victoria 3796 Australia
Email info@GlobalPublishingGroup.com.au

Printed in China

For further information about orders:
Phone: +61 3 9739 4686 or Fax +61 3 8648 6871

To those souls who will never settle for less than they can be, do, share, and give.

We dedicate this book to you, who made the decision to pick the book up in the first place and it's you who has taken the time to read and learn from this book.
This tells us, that you are 'serious' about your future, never making the mistakes we made, and it will be you who will successfully liberate small business from the plague of mediocrity.

"The future has many names.
For the weak, it's unattainable.
For the fearful, it's unknown.
For the bold, it's ideal."

VICTOR HUGO

Acknowledgements

We would like to express our gratitude to the many people who saw us through this book; it has been immensely difficult to relive the story. While this book is written about the depths of a journey, from it came so many lessons which we believe could assist a huge proportion of people who are in business today. We all go into business for all the right reasons, but our path can become very disjointed. Stay strong and focused.

In business, people such as Alex Mandossian, Tony Robbins, Mal Emery, Liz and Matt Raad, Jon Penberthy, Jay Conrad Levinson, Sir Richard Branson, Oprah Winfrey, Stephen Covey, Brian Tracey, T Harv Eker, Robert Kyosaki, Jay Abrahams, Dan Kennedy, Brad Sugars, Steve Plummer and Pete Godfrey have been important sources for our success.

Most significantly, we'd like to thank our son Joshua who walked through the journey with us and always gave back unconditional love, Lorraine's darling parents who were a pillar of strength, Teresia Matthews, Marilyn Hanzalik, Vivien and John Coolen, Adrienne and Paul Dudley, Kim Kershaw, Amanda and Peter Steele.

To all those who allowed us their time to talk things over, read, wrote, offered comments, allowed us to quote their remarks and assisted in the editing, proofreading and design.

A huge "thank-you" to our publisher Global Publishing Group and their supportive team.

And finally, we thank our students for their ongoing support and trust in allowing us to guide them to future success.

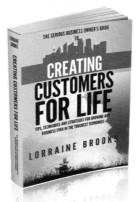

Contents

Foreword

The book you hold in your hands could change your life.

Positive, permanent change can happen in a single moment. Mother Theresa found this to be true. And it was true for Mahatma Gandhi. It was also true for the late Steve Jobs. Billionaire Sir Richard Branson has had many moments.

So many people who read this book will consume the words and then the 'shovel of reality' will hit their foreheads and all the possibilities of a bigger, brighter, bolder future will disintegrate.

I challenge you to look at possibility differently from this moment forward. This is your time. Your time is now. Any time you think something is IMPOSSIBLE… write it down. Just do it. Write it down so it pours out of your mind and you see it on paper.

And then I want to you to do something that's super simple, but super powerful.

Look at the word, IMPOSSIBLE, with a different point of view. Because out of every impossibility comes a possibility that's silently begging you to break its way out.

IMPOSSIBLE is really → I'M POSSIBLE!

And so it is with your moments of impact you have on your friends, family and the most influential person you encounter every day you look in the mirror – YOU!

It matters not whether you are an entrepreneur, a start-up, have spent decades in a business, or anywhere in between; whether you are partially involved in a business or involved every day of your business life; whether you build a business for the excitement of the challenge, or whether it is to pay for lifestyle. To produce something truly successful, the same rules apply to all.

This book isn't a turgid or forensic examination of the rights and wrongs of each situation; rather, it seeks to get into minds of the people behind the business disaster and ask, "Why on earth did they do that?" It pinpoints pitfalls and highlights destructive personality traits, helping readers avoid making similar mistakes.

It is designed to show you how to become extremely savvy, to be able to make outstanding decisions and to get clear about what you really need to put in place to operate a successful business. It will also guide you through the fundamentals of the things you need to have in place to safeguard yourself and those around you.

I'm so happy to recommend this book, as the authors do whatever it takes (WIT), who never give up, and have given you such invaluable first-hand information and lessons that is not easily accessible.

It is an inspiring read and one that will make you want to leap out of your comfort zone and take action. It's your turn to convert IMPOSSIBLE into I'M POSSIBLE. I encourage you to do that daily!

Lorraine and Robert have turned an emotional and complex subject into something easy to read, understand, and to learn from the lessons provided within. As they explain, the book provides you with both a decision making shield and sword. The shield is intended to protect you from making bad decisions. The sword is your most powerful influential weapon. Use it for good.

Alex Mandossian

CEO & Founder
MarketingOnline.com

What Other Experts Are Saying

I would like to personally congratulate you for investing in this valuable book... *Moment of Impact.*

This is a book about turning adversity into opportunity and frankly, that is where most great breakthroughs come from. Would we prefer to skip the adversity? I am sure we would.

However, it seems it is almost a prerequisite to change for the good.

The thing about adversity is not whether it will happen; it's when it will happen. It's how you handle that adversity that determines the future.

I believe the so-called 'impossible' is actually very possible, if you are willing to work very hard, and if you realize that problems and adversity can become opportunities.

When a disaster strikes most people curl up in the corner timidly doing nothing. This is not what has happened here. This book will teach you about agility and strength. It will arm you with the protection you need when running a business.

So many books these days are abstract and focus on theory alone without any real world examples. Lorraine and Rob use their own experiences to highlight their points. This brings them to life, makes them real and shows us how we can use them to improve our own businesses.

Whatever your position is in your business, whatever you want in life, whatever you are shooting for, the chances are that someone else is already living it. They have already invested years of their life and probably hundreds of thousands of dollars, they've made lots of mistakes, learnt from them and eventually succeeded. So why would you want to waste your own time, money and effort through 'trial and error' when you can fast-track your success by learning from 'someone else's experience'?

As you read this book, you will be sharing in the wisdom Lorraine and Rob have gained over their years in business. They have worked with business ventures of every kind, condition and category; the examples and methods shown will help remind you that, no matter the desperation of your current status, you are not alone.

I am honoured to recommend this book, as the authors are fighters who have never given up and have given you such invaluable first-hand information and lessons that is not easily accessible.

Mal Emery

Australia's Millionaire Maker

Lorraine and Rob are true Champions.

They have experienced an incredible business and life journey, and shown all the qualities that make champions great – intention, commitment, focus, discipline and incredible grit and determination in the face of challenge.

But what we admire most about them, and this book, is that they have the courage and compassion to open up about an experience that most people desperately try to hide.

In our greatest challenges, are the greatest opportunities to learn and grow. Lorraine and Rob have looked back at their experience without judgement and with the intention of gaining from their experience and sharing those lessons in the hope that you can benefit.

As business investment and online business advisors, we have helped many people get through similar situations and move into the online business world where the opportunities for growth and freedom in business are almost unlimited.

If you are thinking about getting into business, then you need to read this book – cover to cover. Learn from their experiences and create a business that supports your health and happiness as well as your wealth!

Liz & Matt Raad

eBusiness Institute
ebusinessinstitute.com.au

This book, *Moment of Impact*, is a must read for anyone who wants more out of life and their business. This could be business related or personal.

I believe that if you're willing to put in the hard work and look for opportunity in every problem or adversary, 'the impossible' can actually become very possible!

The funny thing is that the same rules for success apply to all of us equally – to those just starting and those who have literally spent decades in business. They apply to entrepreneurs, start-ups and seasoned veterans. Those who are caught up with the excitement of the challenge and those who are just making extra money to support a lifestyle.

If your goal is to produce something truly successful, you will benefit from the lessons laid out in this book.

Lorraine and Robert didn't set out to produce a forensic examination of each situation, but simply wanted to show how they fell into pitfalls, to try and explain their thought process and why they were caught in each situation and how they went on to survive it.

Their goal is to help the reader anticipate these traps in business and avoid making these costly and potentially devastating mistakes.

I believe that through reading the book, you will gain valuable insights that will help you make better, more informed decisions and most importantly be able to safeguard your investment in your business.

I have the greatest respect for Lorraine and Robert, a couple of fighters who never quit! By writing this honest and open account of their experience, they've provided valuable, first-hand information that you just won't see anywhere else.

I'm honoured to recommend this book, as it is sure to give you the inspiration to grow, to leave your comfort zone and to take action – armed with valuable business knowledge few other people possess.

You'll find this book easy to read, understand and learn from. It is a book every business owner on the planet should read and it is my hope it enables many business to succeed where they may have fallen and saves families from the heartbreak and stress associated with a business failure.

I do hope you enjoy it as much as I did. It will help you immensely on your journey to success.

Jon Penberthy

International Video Marketer & YouTube Expert

Lorraine and Rob are savvy entrepreneurs whose passion for helping others runs deep. We first met at a USA Mastermind and since then I've seen first-hand the impact Lorraine and Rob have had on changing business owners' lives. This book is jam packed full of wisdom and a must-read if you're serious about being successful.

Darren J Stephens

No. 1 International Bestselling Author
Millionaires & Billionaires Secrets Revealed

Prelude

It was like an apocalyptic movie. We discovered that there was a massive comet coming towards us. An Earth-shattering comet. Everything we'd achieved, every hour we'd toiled, every dream we'd worked for and those we'd realized – was soon going to be completely irrelevant. The comet just kept coming closer and closer.

Right up until the last couple of days, we still held on to the hope that we could divert it – that a miracle would happen… But it kept right on coming – It was three days away, then two, then 24 hours, 12 hours, six hours, two hours – And then BOOM!

Life as we knew it changed completely, at that moment of impact.

We picked ourselves up warily, brushed the dust off and peered at each other. We were still breathing. Then we began to slowly, warily look around. As the dust cleared, the destruction began to appear. Everything was decimated. Nothing was left. Nothing at all. The plant and equipment, the staff we'd treated like family, our family home, even many of our good friends were gone…

All we could do was to walk away. Climb up out of the massive crater at the point of impact and start again.

I read somewhere that "It's not what happens to you, it's how you deal with what happens to you," and the true meaning really sinks in when something major does happen! You have many choices at that moment and in the subsequent days, weeks and months those choices and decisions shape the rest of your life.

You could be forgiven for saying life isn't fair and that it wasn't your fault, but in reality, we know that we are responsible for everything that happens to us. We are all happy to accept the accolades and responsibility for our successes, so if you accept responsibility for your failure as well you suddenly realize that you can take charge and you are responsible for your future. It's in your hands! That of course doesn't make it any easier to achieve, but it does make it easier to reason!

At the end of the day, we had gained but one thing – something more valuable than everything we'd lost – wisdom. The kind of wisdom that's etched into your soul through struggle. Through blood, sweat and tears.

The objective of this book is to share that wisdom with other business owners like you – in the hope that it will help you avoid having to experience your moment of impact!

Some people say that adversity makes you stronger and more resilient. But on reflection, we'd say it is better to do without the adversity and learn the lessons before the bad stuff happens to you!

CHAPTER 1

Just a Bad Dream, or a Dream That Turned Bad?

CHAPTER 1

Just a Bad Dream, or a Dream That Turned Bad?

I thought it would all go away when I woke up and opened my eyes. Just another bad dream. But the look on Robert's face told me it was all too real.

If you've never lost your family home, it would be hard to truly understand the feeling. Your last day in the beautiful home you designed and built, with everything just the way you wanted it – preparing to be banished to the wilderness – a rental, somebody else's property, having to adapt to whatever is there, staying until they renovate or sell – completely at the mercy of the landlord.

I walked slowly into my beautiful spacious, open plan kitchen and put the kettle on, running my hand along the marble benchtop. It all seemed surreal. A great feeling of emptiness descended on me – a part of me was relieved to be through the stress of the foreclosure, but mainly it was just overwhelming grief. We had been forced to leave our family home, forever.

Coffee in hand, I sank into a leather couch, staring ahead. Robert was silent. A crisis always brings out the best or worst in people and I'd have to believe it brought out our best. Through all the grief and worry, we hadn't even started to turn on each other. We'd stayed strong as a family, facing the storm together.

They say that it is only through immense pressure that diamonds are formed – and we felt we'd really been given the opportunity to shine. We did have disagreements, but our relationship and our love for each other was unbreakable and we emerged stronger and more united.

My thoughts drifted back to how it all started. I pondered the reasons we'd left high paying jobs in the corporate world and risked everything; the corporate politics we'd had to endure, the idiots we'd had to tolerate, and the belief that we could do better and be the master of our own destiny…

We'd left all that nearly eight years ago. Good grief, eight years of hard work had led to this point – where we'd not only lost everything we'd worked to achieve, but everything we'd worked for prior to that. Our life savings.

Why did we ever go down this path?

Thinking back to those corporate days, more than anything I remember the weariness. The stress of making sure the children were well looked after until we could pick them up. Dragging ourselves home, well after dark, physically and emotionally exhausted. The process being very robotic.

The Original Dream

After years of working in the corporate world, Robert in banking, myself in Information Technology, we dreamed of something we could 'retire into'. Spending five or six days a week for years on end, dressing in suits, rushing to and from the office in peak-hour traffic, in summer, winter, in the cold and rain – getting home exhausted after nightfall, we'd seriously begun to tire of it.

The long stressful hours, with the pressure of having to deliver continuously, even when you feel ill or depressed, starts to eat away at you. There's no escape – we all aspire to climb the corporate ladder, to get that promotion – but all we're getting is even more pressure, longer hours and more stress.

Our definition of success and our dreams had changed over time, from wanting to reach those top level positions, to yearning an alternative – something that would still pay for our lifestyle, but allow us to escape the pressure cooker we were stuck in.

So when we dreamed of our own business, we dreamed of something as far as possible removed from this pressure cooker that had become our world. Nature, perhaps tourism. A nice little country pub or winery – or maybe a horticultural business. There is an altruistic side to most of us, and a business that provided pleasure to others and brightened their lives, while also providing a small reduction in global warming, seemed to tick all the boxes.

It was as far away from our experience of the corporate world as possible, and that was extremely appealing.

When you focus on something with all your energy, the law of attraction comes into play and you begin to see those opportunities everywhere – and we did.

Now you must understand that although we were dreamers, we were by no means flippant or foolish, we were astute buyers. We'd got to reasonably high management levels in the corporate world by working hard and being thorough. We'd managed large projects, so we were used to making sure every base was covered, leaving nothing to chance – and that's how we approached our business acquisition.

The 'Cash Out' Curse

It was during this search for our dream business, that we learned our first real world business lesson – never take cash out of a business you want to sell. An extraordinary number of the businesses we looked at had purchase prices that couldn't be substantiated – because the owners were taking cash out, under the table. The businesses looked enticing, some of them were possibly solid, profit-earning businesses – but there was no way to substantiate the income they claimed to have. We were certainly not going to hand over our life savings on the word of a business owner who had already displayed a level of dishonesty – cash out is, after all, tax evasion.

The owners of most of the businesses we assessed had unrealistic expectations of the sale price. Most were working long hours and had not systematized anything in their business, so they were in effect, just selling a job. We could see no reason to buy another one, having already left two in the corporate world.

So that really narrowed down the real opportunities, to one: A nursery.

How could we go wrong in horticulture? We loved trees!

We assessed a lot of the dream opportunities that we were attracted to and one in particular, stood out – A horticulture business. The numbers added up – we could tick all the boxes. And we loved the idea – this was about as far from corporate Australia as we could get. Close to nature, growing, nurturing trees and selling them to a long term, loyal group of customers. How could we possibly go wrong?

Now Robert and I are great believers in complete commitment to any decision we make – and we fully expect to be tested or challenged when we're on the right path so we didn't let the obstacles to buying this business discourage us, but the first obstacle was a rather large one – the business was out of our price range.

Even using all the equity in our house as collateral, we were still well short of the asking price.

LESSONS:

The process of assessing businesses taught us that as a business owner, you must start with the end in mind. If you intend to build your business up as a saleable asset that can fund your retirement or to use as a stepping-stone to something even bigger, you must structure it so that it is attractive to buyers. In doing so, you will build a more profitable entity, that gives you a better quality lifestyle.

Remember that it is truly a buyers' market and becoming more of one every year, as thousands of baby boomers put their businesses on to the market to retire. Only a very small percentage are even saleable.

According to the Australian Institute of Business Brokers in their report 'AIBB Small Business Sales Index, The State Of The Australian Market', member brokers assessed over 82,000 businesses being offered for sale in 2014 and sold just 2,000. That's just 2.4%.

Comments from their brokers in the report give us a good idea of the reasons:

> *"Overly cautious and influenced by negative political and economic media comment."*

> *"Slow, buyers are very nervous."*

> *"Many small businesses are trying to sell, however due to the number of hours they work and the lack of profitability, buyers are difficult to find."*

> *"Tough buyers' market with scarcity of quality listings available."*

> *"More inquiry, although owners are not putting good businesses on the market."*

> *"Extremely tough as vendor expectations are for too high a price and too few buyers to create competitive tension."*

"There is significant appetite for solid, profitable businesses showing signs of growth; however, these businesses seem to be very rare. Many large businesses (i.e. turnover $1m+) seem to have contracted over the last 3 years making it a difficult proposition to achieve an acceptable sale price."

"There is continuing caution by lending institutions. Reasonable enquiry level, but pricing expectations between vendor and buyer is remarkably different."

"Buyers are still cautious and looking for a bargain, but good well priced businesses are still attracting interest."

Selling a business because it's become difficult to run, due to financial problems or government regulations is almost impossible to do under the current climate. Even businesses that are profitable, but require the owners to work long hours are virtually unsaleable – except to buyers who want to pick them up for a bargain basement price, systematize them and turn them into a valuable asset.

Here are some steps to take if you're thinking of selling your business:

1. Most experts will advise you to start out by getting a business appraisal. You could approach your accountant, or go straight to a large broker or investment banking firm. Brokers who are AIBB members are preferable as they have the current market data and are able to advise you based on their knowledge of the market. You will then have an idea of your businesses potential value and what you will need to do to maximise your chances of a sale.

   It's important to know that the steps you will take to improve the saleability of your business will ultimately make it a better, more profitable enterprise – so it is well worth the time and money you'll invest.

2. If your books aren't in order, now is the time to correct that. For a buyer to properly evaluate your business, they'll need at least three years' worth of financial information. Statements prepared and reviewed by your accountant will carry a lot more weight than something you've just prepared yourself.

3. Your financial statements need to reflect the true profitability of your business. A lot of businesses take cash out 'under the table' and while this may be profitable in the short term, it does nothing for the value of your business and will turn serious buyers away. It's also illegal.

   Expenses that are really perks, such as the business paying off your car lease, should be reflected as profit, while one off large capital outlays or expenses like relocating to a new office, should also be highlighted, with receipts to support these claims. Highlight any one off or unusually high expenses that are not the norm.

4. Systematize everything you possibly can. There is much more detail on this in other chapters in the book, but as you can see from the business broker's comments, buyers reject businesses that require the owners to work long hours. The only way you can reduce the hours you must spend in the business is to systematize every process, including training.

   As you systematize your business, you will also systematize your sales, marketing and customer retention programs – and this will result in a healthy increase in sales and profitability.

5. Make sure you have a system to accurately access and measure the KPIs (key performance indicators) in every area of your business and that you can monitor them remotely. This allows you to keep your finger on the pulse and jump in quickly if things are going astray. All staff and management must have clearly defined, easily measurable, and agreed measurements for their job performance.

This will also introduce accountability to staff, as they know you are monitoring the business – keeping them honest and on track.

6. Make sure your operation gives a great first impression to any potential buyer. If your office, showroom or plant are generally untidy and appear disorganised, now is the time to change that. That first impression may make a huge difference in the price a buyer is willing to pay.

   If customers or clients are accessing these areas, getting them in order could well result in an increase in sales. This may be a reflection of your mindset or maybe you are oblivious to it.

7. Make sure your operation is fully compliant. Ensure all permits are kept up-to-date and you are doing whatever is necessary to be Occupational Health & Safety (OH&S) compliant. An astute buyer should look for this, as if these areas are neglected and something goes wrong, it can result in fines or even jail terms for the owners or management.

   Being fully compliant also makes it possible to tender to supply government agencies and corporate clients, so it is a worthwhile exercise. We go into this in more detail in future chapters.

Getting a business ready for sale will take a lot of your time and resources. It's important not to try and rush this, but to steadily implement everything over time – particularly systematization: just choose one area at a time and systematize and document it properly, involving staff in the process, so they are willing participants. Then move on to the next area.

It's important to minimise the impact of this work on your day-to-day running of the business. If you drop the ball here, you will lose customers and your sales and profit will suffer, resulting in your business becoming less saleable.

My Notes / Thoughts

CHAPTER 2

Achieving the Impossible

CHAPTER 2

Achieving the Impossible

Any bank manager would have rightly laughed at our proposal. We simply couldn't afford the business we were determined to own. We had no experience in business and certainly none in horticulture, so, on paper, we didn't have a lot going for us.

But when you're in the finance industry, you know the language they speak and what they look for in a proposal.

And Robert was a 30-year veteran of finance, holding senior management roles in a number of financial institutions – and his job had been to lend as much money as he could to his clients. He also worked in the business finance sector, specialising in business-banking finance, corporate banking finance and development finance, so this was right up his alley.

That didn't make it a walk in the park, but Robert did know which brokers were best to target and he had a good contact in that sector who was able to get the loan approved. To make it easier and move it along faster, Robert took the time to assist with the loan application and suggest terms of the loan for the finance broker.

The amount the bank had proposed was still not sufficient to purchase the business; we'd need additional finance of some kind for that. There would also be no money available to run the business or buy additional business assets we might need, such as motor vehicles and equipment. So Robert negotiated directly with the bank manager and arranged for an overdraft and asset finance facility to be part of the deal.

We also negotiated vendor finance with the owner who had become very motivated as the sale became more a reality.

A buyer's market

It's been a buyer's market for small businesses in Australia for some time and had we been better negotiators we probably could have bought at a much better price. But this was never going to be a bargain – it was a premium business at a premium price.

We were however able to squeeze a deal of a different kind out of him. Vendor finance. As a motivated buyer with few offers on the table, he was willing to take a portion of the money in quarterly instalments over five years at 8½% interest. The owner had no problem at all with this and this made up the shortfall we had from the amount the bank would loan us. We were over the line! As part of the contract of sale we included a non-competition clause for the five year term of the vendor finance. So the seller was precluded from starting a similar business until he had received the full purchase price. By including such a clause the seller would be unlikely to break it as he would not receive the balance of the monies outstanding and may be forced to forfeit the monies already paid. By deferring part of the purchase price over five years allows an astute business owner to use the business to pay off the loan. If the business can be grown then the additional revenue can often more than cover the repayments on the vendor finance. Also inflation reduces the real amount to repay the loan which is an additional bonus.

Time to crack open the champagne

We were elated! This was really meant to happen and the universe was opening it all up for us. We were going to be Free – free of the corporate drudgery, free of office politics, free of the horrible people we were forced to work with. We were going to work on our terms – hire the people we liked, fire those we didn't, work the hours we wanted to, out in the fresh air, surrounded by nature – It was a dream come true, or so we thought…

As the bubbly flowed and we patted ourselves on the back, we recounted how thoughtful the owner had been, offering to spend a full three months full time with us, to ensure we really knew our way around the business. That was invaluable. We'd not only found a great business, but it seemed we'd also gained a friend, a mentor!

We admired the staff and appreciated the great team the owner had managed to assemble – and that was certainly what you needed to be successful in business – a team who were fully engaged, firing together. A team you could trust!

We remember being as excited as children shaking the boxes under the Christmas tree before the big day. This was going to be an incredible ride!

LESSONS:

The process of buying really taught us that as business guru Jay Abraham says: "In real estate and in business, the money is made in buying at the right price." So the negotiating process is important.

It also taught us that in the euphoria of a sale, many promises are made and believed, but it is necessary to document everything and as with other contracts, penalties must be specified for non-performance.

When one party fails to do what they have promised, there must be consequences.

It is vital that when you buy a business, you ensure that you have enough capital to also run the business – otherwise you could very quickly run into cash-flow problems – and remember, this is the number one cause of small business failure in Australia.

We realize this is not common knowledge, and most people new to business would be unaware of it. Your best course of action would be to seek out a professional business broker and finance broker. You'll find good ones in most major cities. Take the time to speak to them about your cash-flow needs, shop around and find the most reliable person you can.

You want someone who has the experience under their belt and takes the time to explain things properly to you. The goal is to ensure you not only have enough money to complete the purchase but you also have enough money to run the business.

Vendor finance is a great option to help you raise the capital you need and as it is very much a buyer's market, so there are a lot of very motivated vendors around.

Using vendor finance is very similar to borrowing from a bank, but the seller leaves some of the purchase price to be repaid over a period of time, after you take over the business. As with everything there are pluses and minuses to using vendor finance.

The downside is that if you fall behind with payments, the seller can reclaim the business, kick you out and then sue you for the balance you owe them.

Some vendors would love this to happen.

The upside is that the seller is taking some of the risk and it is a great way to lock them out of starting a competing business. Your vendor finance contract should include a clause that says the seller will forfeit all monies due under the vendor finance agreement if they start a competing business or form an alliance with a competitor.

If you make the payments, it is a normal business arrangement.

One piece of advice: do not agree too quickly to pay the seller interest on the vendor finance loan. If the vendor wants the sale badly enough, there is a probability he will agree to interest free terms.

My Notes / Thoughts

CHAPTER 3

In the Cold Light of Day

CHAPTER 3

In the Cold Light of Day

Working our new business was a sobering experience. Our euphoria quickly disappeared.

The first thing that was hammered home was our complete lack of knowledge of the industry. We knew trees and plants, but we had no idea of what a *Melaleuca linarafolia* or *Angophera costata* were – and customers referred to plants by their botanical names. It was almost like learning another language.

Rob realized that despite being a senior bank manager and advising business owners on their businesses, what he actually knew about running a business would probably fit on the back of a postage stamp. We were really getting a hands on crash course .

We started to become overwhelmed very quickly with wages, withholding tax, BAS, superannuation payments – talk about being thrown into the deep end. To make things worse, there were no systems at all in either the nursery or the office. You had to know how to do everything there.

True to his word, the former owner came in every day – not full time as we'd anticipated, but at least he was there to help us through our crash course in botany and business!

We'd drag ourselves home after work, just as exhausted as we'd ever been in the corporate world, but with a whole lot of homework to boot.

Rob was determined to speak the language of the industry, so he would learn ten new botanical names every day while driving to and from work. He often had no idea what the plants actually looked like, but he knew it was just necessary to be able to communicate in the language of the industry.

There were times when we thought that we would never get the hang of it, but perseverance has its own rewards and eventually it started to make sense.

What have we done?

We asked ourselves many times "What have we got ourselves into?" though we did our best not to show our dismay to each other, or to voice our anxiety too much – we were committed and the last thing either of us wanted to do was to discourage the other.

But deep in our hearts, we both felt a sense of self-doubt and even dread. "What if things go wrong?" we'd often ask.

But when you have everything on the line and it is down to you to make it work, you ultimately find a way. The business wasn't the issue in the early days – it was us – whether we had the ability to make it work.

We had to keep going, keep busy and keep the dark cloud of doubt at bay…

A solid foundation

We put a lot of thought and effort into setting up a solid foundation for our business. We wanted to make sure it was structured properly to maximise our profits and minimise our taxation liabilities. We had enough business knowledge to at least know that the legal entity of the business should be structured properly.

So we sought out a good accountant. We knew that somebody with an intimate knowledge in business and taxation law would make a big difference to our ability to keep the money we'd worked so hard for.

Shhhhh – keep it quiet!

When you take over a new business, you expect to keep the customers and the income – that's what you pay the money for. So it's extremely important to understand that a lot of the customer 'goodwill' can actually be tied to the previous owner and not the business. Proudly announcing 'New Management' can make those loyal customers wary and give competitors a chance to take them away. You can have a disaster on your hands before you even start!

In our case, the previous owner was a personality in the industry and a lot of the trade came from relationships he'd formed with customers over time, so we had to be careful not to announce the sale until we'd shown them that there'd be continuity in the products, prices and level of service they'd become accustomed to.

The owner agreed and kept news of the sale very quiet.

Relationships with key staff are equally important. It's almost impossible to keep the news of the sale from them, so you have to move quickly to build relationships with them and make them feel comfortable with the new arrangement.

The last thing we needed was all that knowledge and expertise walking out the door and going across to the competition. So we took great pains to get to personally know the people we were going to work with and build some rapport with them.

So far, so good

By the end of the first month, we were finally settling in. We were confident that our accountant had set up our business to protect our interest; the previous owner was helping as he promised, the transition was going smoothly and we felt we were getting to know staff like family.

We were going to be just fine…

LESSONS:

By not advertising the change of ownership we managed to maintain the integrity of the business and by keeping the staff, there was continuity of contact with the people in the business.

We did not change a thing in the business; it was 'business as usual'.

We are always amazed that someone would buy a successful business and pay money for the goodwill, only to change everything because they think they know better than the seller. If someone has built a successful business they must be doing something right. If you have ideas on how to improve, wait and see exactly what works and what doesn't. Only then make small changes and monitor how successful they are.

The exception to this is when the business isn't going well and you have picked it up for a bargain. Then it may be prudent to put your own face on it immediately – to show it is now under new management and things are going to be done properly from this point on.

But in our case, we were buying a successful operation – so only when we understood the clients and the dynamics of the business and the industry did we make changes. When we did make them, it was slowly at first.

So we'd done everything right at this stage and it was starting to pay off. The important things we learned were:

- Engaging a good accountant to ensure your business is structured correctly to maximise your potential income earnings and minimise your tax liabilities.

- Understanding relationships are extremely important in business – A lot of the 'goodwill' of the business could be tied to relationships with the owner, so those relationships must be fostered. Understanding that relationships with staff are also vital to your success – you need to maintain those relationships to prevent their knowledge, expertise and relationships with customers from walking out the door and going to your competition.

- Always make sure the seller signs an agreement not to compete, and also non-solicitation agreement. This effectively prevents the seller from setting up a competing business for a set period of time, within a specified geographic area. The agreement should also specify 'direct or non-direct competition', also preventing the seller from becoming an employee of a competing business.

- A non-solicitation agreement prevents the seller from recruiting employees for a competing business for a set period of time. These must be very detailed and specific documents including a specific list of employees, to ensure the seller hasn't already recruited key employees before the document was signed.

- Finally the contract should specify that the seller agrees to pay the buyer's solicitor fees to pursue the case in the event of a breach of the contract by the seller.

- A buyer must do everything possible to maintain and profit from the goodwill they paid for when they invest their hard earned cash into a new business.

My Notes / Thoughts

CHAPTER 4

A Taste of Reality

CHAPTER 4

A Taste of Reality

It seemed just like another Monday, our fifth week in the office. We were really getting into the swing of things. Robert had been practising the botanical names and was even sounding like a bit of an expert – we were sure he'd be up-to-speed in another two months, when Paul had finished mentoring us. We were enjoying our time with Paul, he wasn't there with us for as many hours as we'd expected, but he was such an expert in the business and so good at explaining things, that we were still satisfied with progress.

We have noticed a pattern with traditional Australian family business. The wife does the bookkeeping irrespective of experience, and the business we'd bought was no exception, so Paul's wife Helen allocated a few days to help me get up to speed with them. Admittedly, it was the last thing I wanted to do, but it made sense to have a way of monitoring the business on a daily basis.

I was to learn later that there was a much better way of managing this and a much more effective way I could spend my time, but in hindsight, it was a good way to get a feel for the business and it certainly made managing future bookkeepers easy.

Robert had spent all Sunday afternoon writing up questions he wanted to ask Paul. He was very keen, but conscious that Paul was ready to move on, so he didn't want to be a bother to him by being unorganised. Robert was really feeling encouraged at the speed with which he'd been learning with Paul as a mentor and he was really looking forward to the week's activities.

We were now coming into winter which is the busy time in the nursery industry. This was a good time for us to start out in business. Some businesses are seasonal so choosing the right time to take them over is often critical. Most horticultural businesses are busiest in the cooler months, as these are the ideal time to plant the products they sell. During our due diligence we were particularly aware of this factor and so we had to buy the business in late autumn or no deal. There would have been little point in purchasing the business in late Spring or Summer as the majority of the year's sales would have gone to the seller and we would have to wait another six to eight months to reap the seasonal benefits.

Paul goes missing

It was a frosty June morning as we turned into the car park and swung in behind the office. Ashley was there as always waiting, a big smile lit up his face when he saw us. It was heart-warming and reassuring.

Despite our lack of knowledge, we were doing ok with the employees and had recognised the value of Ashley to the business. If he left we would have been in deep trouble as he knew all the clients, suppliers and staff well. So we made an offer to Ashley of a significant bonus if he stayed with us for 12 months, which should be enough time for us to complete the takeover.

Fortunately, he agreed and so he was secured for a year – which gave us a huge amount of comfort. But we still had much to learn and we needed Paul's mentorship – and really looked forward to it each day. So when he went missing, it was a huge blow to us.

It started out like any other day. Robert unlocked the office door and we poured in and headed straight for the kitchen to get the jug going for some coffee. Other employees began to trickle in, slowly bringing the office and nursery to life.

Coffee in hand, I switched on the computer and loaded up MYOB to go through the books again. Robert was looking a little impatient. Paul was unusually late this morning – a bit out of character for him.

I must have got lost in my thoughts, because when I looked up at the clock, it was already 9:30. Robert was pacing the floor, looking more and more agitated every minute. It was really not like him to be late, so I asked Ashley to give him a call – see if there were any problems.

He did not answer.

The day dragged on, with unanswered calls to Paul every hour. Where could he possibly be?

Robert had been so focused on the questions he was going to ask him, that he could not even start anything else.

And so reality set in.

Three more days of no Paul and we became increasingly worried.

Friday morning he finally breezed in without a worry in the world and turned on his usual charm. We knew our mentorship was as good as over. Our mentor had his money and was obviously tired of coming in. We were now effectively on our own.

At least business was good. Orders were being delivered at a steady pace. Through my office window, I could see our truck going out, laden with plants over and over again. I began to wonder if I should perhaps give these clients a reminder to pay their invoices, so I went back into my accounting program to try and find them.

I could see a few invoices there, which was natural as we were coming into peak season… But the amount that had been invoiced for the month seemed disproportionate to the amount of stock going out.

Houston we have a problem!

Then it hit me: in the rush to settle the purchase of the business before the peak order season there had been a mix-up. In the days before the change of ownership Paul had invoiced some of the clients, but not delivered the stock. These sales had not been removed from the amount we had agreed to pay for the stock. If the stock had been adjusted at settlement this error would not have occurred and we would have just paid less for the stock in the purchase price. We should have picked this up, but being new to the business, and with so many other things to think about, we overlooked it. Had we not picked it up then we would have been in real trouble as the value was just shy of $200,000.

It could have been devastating and meant the end of the business. We'd been thrown in the deep end at the busiest time of the year and we were struggling to keep our head above water. Fortunately Paul refunded all the money when we pointed it out to him. In the rush he had forgotten about the advance sales invoices and transferred the funds to our bank account when he received them.

As we were new to the business, we had no idea this was happening. Nor did the clients. They had ordered and paid for stock and they just wanted it delivered.

The existing staff of course just obliged the client and delivered the stock when they were shown the receipts.

It was something every buyer should check when they take over a business– advanced invoicing! Paul had invoiced and in some instances been paid well in advance for stock that was just being delivered. One of the reasons for buying the business was the advanced orders the seller had shown us. So not only had we used these advanced orders as an expected source of income for the year ahead, we had effectively paid for them in the purchase price.

The amount of the advance payments was substantial: almost $200,000. We were already running lean having borrowed heavily to get into the business and this additional amount could have been the straw that broke the camel's back.

The original inventory we received when we took over included all the stock that had been invoiced but not delivered. If we had not picked it up it almost certainly would have resulted in the business failing within three months.

LESSONS:

We thought we'd done our due diligence properly on the business, but we learned that the devil is really in the detail. We checked the stock we were paying for with the business, but we made a presumption that it was unencumbered. We were wrong. You have to be very thorough when buying a business – one mistake like this could bring the whole thing crashing down.

In hindsight, we also should have formalised the handover and training, with payment held until it was completed. This of course is much harder to do when you have vendor finance, as the seller has already effectively agreed to a late payment of funds.

But overall, anything agreed to should be formalised in writing with very little left to chance. Agreements made on a handshake are much easier to break, with few consequences.

Probably the biggest mistake we made was allowing too little time to buy and understand the business. As it was a seasonal business we had to settle when we did. Also remember the seller knows the intricacies of the business, so make sure you ask the right questions.

The Latin phrase *caveat emptor* means 'let the buyer beware' should ring in your mind. Be wary and use experts to help you cover these possible eventualities.

The bankruptcy graveyard is littered with honest people who innocently trusted those they were dealing with and did not make sure everything was documented and signed. When we make assumptions, we leave ourselves open to unscrupulous people who plan to profit at our expense.

Always plan with that in mind. Take people at their word when you can easily afford to lose the amount of money at risk in that transaction and not before. Don't gamble your future and that of your family by making an assumption and not checking the detail.

Here are some other details that need your attention when you buy a business:

1. The goodwill you are paying for is largely determined by a multiple of recurring profits that the business generates. Many business owners however, do not draw a wage, corrupting the financials. In this case, the 'goodwill' you are paying for is not genuine – as the business requires somebody to work at no charge to generate those profits. To calculate the true profit of this business and the goodwill, a salary must be added to the expenses at market rate.

   While it may be acceptable to not draw a wage if you are simply buying a job – if you want anything more, it is not realistic. If you ever intend systematizing the business so you can step back from the day-to-day running, you will have to hire somebody to take on that role. You may then find that the business is not profitable at all.

2. The structure of the existing business may impact on the transfer of some of the assets and liabilities of the business. For instance, if the seller is an individual or partnership and there

are vehicles under hire-purchase or lease, the loan contract should be in their name or names; and the vehicles and liability for them will effectively remain with the seller.

This means you will have to have an agreement to transfer them or be able to buy or lease replacements.

3. Find out the real reason the seller is selling the business. Retirement or family sickness are the most common reasons given for somebody to want to discontinue running a business, but are they the real reasons?

   Has the seller seen something that alarmed them, such as a multinational or large national competitor moving in to their area? Or is the product or service they offer being superseded or becoming completely redundant? – or are a large number of their staff in the process of moving over to a competitor? Are new planned governmental regulations going to dramatically cut their profit margin? Some due diligence on the market and competition will really pay dividends and could save you losing your hard earned cash.

4. Is the business you're looking at in a 'sunrise' or 'sunset' industry? A sunrise industry is one that is new or relatively new, fast growing and expected to peak sometime in the future. Many tech industries are in their sunrise stages, including social media marketing, software as a service, cloud computing, intelligent home design, even space travel.

   Probably the best example of a sunset industry is video and DVD rentals. Other examples of sunset industries are some forms of media like newspapers, film cameras and film, and analogue equipment. Companies that were in sunset industries and didn't evolve, like Kodak and Blockbuster are no longer in business.

It is worth making sure that the product or service the business specializes in is not about to be superseded. Even profitable, systematized businesses in sunset industries only have a limited shelf life.

5. Who are their customers and clients and how stable is their income? Or is a sizeable part of the business dependent on a 'boom and bust' industry like mining? For example, many businesses in rural Western Australia and Perth were dependant on mine workers and while the iron ore sales were booming, they were highly profitable. When prices fell and mines closed down, a lot of these companies folded.

   Now if you were unlucky enough to have assessed one of these businesses just before worldwide demand for iron ore fell, it would have looked good. The figures would have been exceptional and the business may have even been perfectly systematised and set up so you only had to spend a few hours a week working. It would have been a dream business. Well for a few months...

   Then your customers would have almost completely disappeared within a few short months and you would have been powerless to stop it happening. All the systems and customer retention programs in the world could not have saved you, because your customers had lost their jobs. And without the time to prepare and plan some kind of diversification, you would have lost your business.

So buying a business should never be a rushed decision. It is your future and your family's future. You need to do as much due diligence as possible and ensure that you're buying genuine goodwill and that the business has a long term future, as does the industry – and you are not dependent on customers working in an industry that has a boom and bust cycle.

There are good and great businesses out there which are bought and sold every day. There are also underperforming businesses that a good operator can turn into a gold mine!

My Notes / Thoughts

CHAPTER 5

Gaining the Essential Knowledge

CHAPTER 5

Gaining the Essential Knowledge

The next two weeks were painful. Robert tried to bluff his way through work, but it became painfully obvious that his knowledge was inadequate.

Realising Ashley's importance, we had offered him a considerable bonus to stay with us for the next year, as it was obvious he did not have the same level of commitment and respect for us that he had for Paul. And having him moving to a competitor and taking all that knowledge was a real possibility and one that honestly terrified us.

Perhaps this had the unwanted effect of making him feel even more important, because he began becoming less and less helpful, until Robert all but gave up relying on him for assistance. Still, he was effective in his role as nursery manager and that took a lot of pressure off us.

But it left us with a dilemma. We couldn't run the business long term, relying on an employee, without having the necessary knowledge ourselves. It made us extremely vulnerable and we could be left without expertise at any moment, which would then quickly translate to lost business, as customers found out they couldn't rely on our expertise any longer. The business had been built on Paul's industry expertise and that was our competitive advantage in the marketplace.

So really, our only choice was for Robert to enrol in a nursery course at night, while I would just have to work a bit harder to hold the business together with Ashley. We were in for a few long months, but anything worthwhile takes time.

So for six months Robert went back to school at night to get a grounding in horticulture. It was tough but certainly worthwhile and it helped Robert really look and sound like an industry expert.

Robert didn't finish the course, there was no need. Nobody ever asked us what educational attainments we had. When he felt that he'd learned everything he needed and he was at the stage where he could confidently deal with clients, he discontinued his course and devoted his time again, to building the business.

Robert really had to focus on building rapport with clients. Paul had established great relationship with them and competitors left them alone, out of respect for Paul. He was a long-term leader in the horticultural industry. The clients were still all with us because we'd managed to keep news of the sale quiet, but that wasn't going to last forever... Word was going to get out sooner or later and if we hadn't taken care of client relationships, there was a very real chance they would move to our more experienced competitors.

Sometimes at night, we'd collapse into our chairs exhausted, wondering why we had made the transition to our own business. We were both still getting home after dark, tired and cranky. It wasn't exactly the life we'd dreamed of and certainly not worth immersing ourselves in a whole lot of debt for.

But we'd started down this path and we weren't quitters, we were damn well going to make a success of this... and we still had that vision in our minds – of building an empire and of doing it our way.

LESSONS:

Your time is extremely valuable – it's the only thing you can't get more of, so it's essential to know what you need to learn and what you can rely on the trusted advisors to know.

The time you spend gaining industry knowledge is time you're not out there getting sales or working on your systems.

In our case, Robert needed a certain amount of industry knowledge to be able to speak with clients and be respected as a knowledgeable supplier – but there was a limit and Robert was smart enough to know when he had gained enough knowledge to move on to other things.

There's a famous quote from Henry Ford that goes: *"Will you kindly tell me, why I should clutter up my mind with general knowledge, for the purpose of being able to answer questions, when I have men around me who can supply any knowledge I require?"*

Ford was an expert in hiring the right people and building good teams, but he did not know a great deal about the engineering that went into making his vehicles. He knew enough to effectively manage his operation and devoted his time to build a huge business empire that is still a leader in the automobile industry over a century later.

Gain the industry knowledge you need, but focus on surrounding yourself with experts you can trust to provide the knowledge you lack.

The best guide I have ever seen to help you ensure you spend your time on the most important tasks is Steven Covey's Time Management Quadrant:

	Urgent	**Non Urgent**
	Quadrant I:	*Quadrant II:*
Important	Urgent & Important	Important, but Not urgent
	Quadrant III:	*Quadrant IV:*
Not Important	Urgent, but Not Important	Not Urgent Or Important

If you're going to be effective in your business, your goal should be to spend as much of your time as possible in Quadrant II – the important, but not urgent quadrant. This is where you do all the maintenance and preparation that stops you having to drop everything to do Quadrant I tasks.

Examples of Quadrant II (important, but not urgent) tasks we did:

- Studying at TAFE to gain industry knowledge.
- Going to training seminars to pick up knowledge and motivation.
- Building rapport with clients and staff – maintaining relationships.
- Putting systems in place in our business so that everybody knew what to do and new staff could easily fit in and become productive.

If we didn't do those Quadrant II tasks, we would have been forced to drop everything and do Quadrant I (Urgent & Important) tasks, like:

- Rushing to try and save contracts when clients pulled out because we obviously didn't know what we were talking about.
- Rushing to see the bank manager to organise another overdraft to keep our cash flow going because we lost work through not having good client relationships.
- Putting off other work to train new staff and make sure they knew what to do, because there are no systems in place to follow.

The simplest way of explaining this is the example of your car. If you don't service it regularly (Quadrant II tasks), you have to drop everything else you're doing and get it fixed when it breaks down on the side of the road, leaving you stranded (Quadrant I task).

The biggest time killer

So why doesn't everybody spend their time in Quadrant II? The reason is Quadrat III – Urgent, But Not Important. Those tasks are the biggest time killers for most of the population, including small business owners. They are tasks which demand your attention right now, but you can and should schedule for an appropriate time.

Here are examples of Quadrant III (Urgent but Non-Important) tasks that are time-traps:

- Tidying up your desk
- Checking and answering emails – this is a common time killer, that can easily be scheduled to be done twice a day.
- Facebook or Skype chat. These are attention grabbing but in most cases, not urgent and people wanting to chat can be politely told that you're busy and will get back to them later. This is probably the biggest time-killer for staff and it's something every business owner needs to bring under control.

The final quadrant, Quadrant IV (Non Urgent, Not Important) is for those activities that yield little or any value. These are activities that are often used for taking a break from time pressured and important activities.

By understanding the time-wasting traps of Quadrant III and eliminating them to spend more time in Quadrant II, we can become much more effective in our business and in our lives.

My Notes / Thoughts

CHAPTER 6

The Buzzards are Circling

CHAPTER 6

The Buzzards are Circling

The wholesale plant industry in Melbourne is competitive – and we knew our competitors would pounce the moment they found out Paul was no longer the owner of our business. Paul had managed to carve himself out a special niche because of his expertise and there was no way we could possibly gain that level of expertise before the word eventually got out.

So we had to build rapport with clients and hope that was enough to get us through.

We'd also banked on providing continuity through keeping key staff like Ashley.

But when news of the change of ownership got out, it spread faster than a bushfire raging through a eucalyptus forest, and the buzzards came circling. Rumours spread like wildfire. Apparently, newcomers have a high failure rate in the horticulture industry and we were given six months. "They'll be out of business very soon" our clients were told. Staff also picked up the rumours and we could feel a difference in the way they treated us. In fact, something we were to find out much later was there were actual monetary bets, placed by numerous business owners on how long we would last!

But this is where our initial hard work paid dividends.

In a relatively short space of time, we'd managed to forge strong enough relationships with clients that they were reluctant to move. We'd also tied up key staff with incentives so despite being worried about their future, they still hung in there.

We'd also developed enough industry knowledge to ease client concerns – so despite the rumours being spread, they still had faith in us. Let's face it, switching suppliers is a hassle nobody really wants to go through, so provided we maintained the same standard of products and services at the same price, we stood a good chance of keeping most clients.

Those long days had ultimately been worthwhile. They had saved our investment. Now we had to build on what we had, work on our business and systematize it – so key staff could run the business and we could really live our dream.

This was something unfortunately Paul had not paid enough attention to. He'd been successful, but had a very hands-on approach. The business really had no systems at all. It relied heavily on Paul and his expertise to succeed. Despite the research we did we'd effectively bought ourselves highly paying jobs. We had listened to the rhetoric of the seller and not focussed on the facts. All the vendor's knowledge was in his head and not where it needed to be – documented in systems.

But with our limited experience, building systems was hard. Where do we start? We needed to standardize the way staff dealt with clients, with ordering, following up to ensure clients were satisfied, getting feedback…

It was very difficult and time-consuming for us to start a new employee in the nursery, in the absence of any system.

Most training was conducted in what's known as the 'tribal' method – (with information passed from 'man-to-man'). A new employee would be told: "Just stick with Stuart for a couple of days and do what he does."

This leads to a lack of consistency, as everybody would do things their way and people will tend to follow the path of least resistance.

The end result is a substandard product and performance.

We started to think about it. It was a massive task, but one we needed to undertake as a matter of urgency. We could never reduce our work hours or expect to take time off until the whole business, from the nursery to the office had been properly systematized.

This is where our corporate background helped. Large companies operate on systems – that is how they become large, so we both had experienced working in systems. So over the next few months, we looked at each process one-by-one, identified the best way of doing it, then documented it and made sure all staff received training.

There was initially some resistance – people generally don't like changing the way they do things. But we pushed and when they began to realize that it actually made their job easier, they quickly conformed.

LESSONS:

Relationships are important in a business and they must be nurtured and maintained. Particularly relationships with your staff, your clients, or your customers. All the systems in the world will not help you if your staff keep jumping ship and taking their expertise to your competitors.

The same is true for customers or clients. Without them, you don't have sales and your business won't last long. The cheapest marketing you will ever do is to your existing clients or customers. You can literally increase sales without spending any money on advertising, by increasing the amount they spend or the frequency in which they buy.

Systems are critical for any business to be able to grow and be a saleable asset and you must find time to address them.

Had we engaged a good, experienced business coach when we took over our nursery operation, that coach would have made us begin to address systems right from day one.

Without systems, there is little consistency in the business or in the quality of products and services. People will naturally take shortcuts to make their jobs easier and to be more productive in the hope of pleasing their employer. They will also push the boundaries like children do at home – and the more they get away with, the more they will try.

Systems allow you to set boundaries and set clear expectations of what your employees are expected to achieve and how they're expected to achieve it.

Systems ensure tasks are performed consistently, regardless of who does them. They ensure new staff can be brought up to speed very quickly and when combined with good reporting (addressed in a later chapter), they ultimately free up the business owner to be able to enjoy life. Systems do not target an individual. They target a role or job within the business, and as such they remove any personal emotion from the process.

Training should be a part of your systems. Staff do not value 'tribal training' and you have no hope of protecting your intellectual property when you train people in that manner. They regard it as their own knowledge, to use for their own benefit, with whoever they choose.

So most training, especially that which is specific to your operations, should be conducted in a formal setting and a value placed on it. An agreement can be drawn up for it, with confidentiality clauses.

Probably the best example of the power of systems is McDonald's.

You've probably heard the saying: *"Anybody can make a better burger than McDonald's, but nobody can make better systems than McDonalds."*

Systems are what make McDonald's franchises worth millions of dollars. They can guarantee the franchisee an income, provided that they follow the systems. The systems also ensure that the owner does not have to be there running the store. Once he has a manager trained, the business literally runs itself. It's a money machine.

Ray Kroc or the McDonald brothers who founded the business did not have to go and spend time training each new cook how to make their burgers – they documented it. They systematized the whole process, right from the point of contact when the counter staff ask, "Would you like fries and a drink with that?", to the way in which the tables are cleaned, once you have finished your meal.

The McDonald's systems ensure consistency – throughout the world. Even in the furthermost corner of the planet, you can walk into any of the 33,000+ McDonald's stores and taste a burger very similar to the one you get around the corner, and eat it in an environment as clean as the one in your local area.

Systems are the difference between the little local takeaway shop on the corner and the global food empire – and systematizing your business is the only way to gain your freedom from long hours of work.

You should address these items when you systematize a business (see following page):

Sales and Marketing

1. **Lead generation** – Including online and offline advertising and social media.
2. **Lead nurturing and conversion** – Regular follow up, informing and educating them leading to a sale.
3. **Planning and strategy** – Continual evaluation of marketing results and new marketing ideas – testing and measuring.
4. **Branding** – Ensuring all marketing material is consistent with your corporate identity.
5. **Lifetime value** – Understand what a client is worth over their lifetime allowing you to know how much you can afford to spend to acquire them.

Operations

1. **General Administration** – Ensuring the business administration runs smoothly and consistently, regardless of whether you're there or not.
2. **Production** – Every business will have different production systems to ensure consistency in the quality of the product or service.
3. **Fulfilment** – Ensuring orders are fulfilled consistently in a timely manner.
4. **Customer service** – Ensuring customer questions and complaints are promptly followed up
5. **Purchasing** – To ensure employees don't go on a spending spree.

Financial Management

1. **Accounting/Reporting** – Ensuring you have real-time information on the financial health of your business.
2. **Invoicing and collections** – Ensuring invoices are sent out on time, follow-ups are made and payments are collected
3. **Accounts payments** – Ensuring staff, suppliers, contractors and taxation payments are consistently made on time.
4. **Planning and Budgeting** – Consistent planning sessions to identify changes in sales, costs, requirements for expansion and plan for them.
5. **Cash-flow management** – Ensuring there is consistency and accountability.

Your Team

1. **The hiring process** – Including advertising, interviewing, reference checking.
2. **Training** – All types of training should be systematised and formalised as much as possible.
3. **Employee reviews and retention** – Keeping employees engaged and getting feedback from them.
4. **Compliance** – Particularly OHS
5. **Outsourcing** – Sourcing and management of outsourced employees and contractors
6. **Exit processes** – Ensuring thorough handovers are conducted to incoming replacements, clearances are signed etc.

If you look at the whole business at once, it can be very intimidating and daunting. The best way to do it is by one area at a time, consistently and thoroughly, then moving on to the next. Some areas can be addressed with appropriate software, while others will require documentation.

Training is an important part of the process, as systems are only good if your staff are trained to use them and there are consequences for not using them.

My Notes / Thoughts

CHAPTER 7

The Hardest Thing You'll Have to Do in Business

CHAPTER 7

The Hardest Thing You'll Have to Do in Business

Through the process of building relationships with our employees, we got to know them so well, they became almost like family to us. After all, they were the key to our success and the key to us ever getting a life.

We decided to keep them informed of our plans and aspirations for the business, as we found new directions we could take it in, so they had a sense of ownership. Goals were set by all divisions and from these the goals formed a working plan. We wanted them to feel like a team, not just a group of employees trying to work out what was happening with the company and if they would continue to be a part of it.

If they were aware of the overall goals and how their tasks contributed to those goals, they would be much more productive and could even suggest ways of improving the process.

We kept an eye out for relevant outside training for them, both personal and business, and tried to get them feeling they were growing a worthwhile career rather than just treading water until something better came along.

We also decided that every time an employee left, we would raise the bar to replace them with someone better. Someone more skilled, with a better attitude. Over the 7½ years we ran the business, we grew it from a small team of five to an organised, structured team of almost 60.

It was always rewarding watching people with raw talent and enthusiasm grow into specialists, with a rewarding career ahead of them. It was sometimes frustrating, working hard to help someone progress, only to discover they didn't really want the job, or they were using the job as a stepping stone for the job they really wanted with another company. It was also sometimes heart-wrenching, as in the case of Alice.

Alice was a promising young lady who truly enjoyed the work and really had green thumbs. The plants she cared for thrived. They grew faster, thicker and more vibrant than plants around them. She had a bubbly personality, an easy person to like, but she had to go…

Despite being such a promising young employee, Alice simply didn't produce. She was literally in a world of her own, pampering a small number of plants she really loved, but never really growing enough to justify the wage we were paying her.

Alice was like family. We really loved her and wanted her to be with us for the long haul. We tried time after time to find ways to engage her and get her working well, but everything failed. She was happy in her own little world and just didn't want to change.

It probably sounds a bit heartless but business is business and not a hobby. When growing plants for sale some have to be sacrificed to maintain the characteristics and quality the buyer expects and wants. Trying to save every plant is a hobby and unfortunately not the prerequisite of a business.

When you run a small business, you can't afford to carry people who aren't producing. You're paying their salary from the gross profit of the business, so sometimes when you have exhausted every other option you have to bite the bullet and let them go. We knew Alice had to go, but we continued to postpone that moment in the hope that somehow, something would change.

The longer we left it, the more difficult it became and the more we thought about it, until it began to give us so much stress we just had to confront it. It fell on Robert's shoulders to deal with it, so Monday morning, he matched into the office with his jaw set, ready to deal with what has become his biggest fear.

It went horribly. Alice broke down in tears and we were all affected. It was really like losing a family member and it was something that haunted Robert for months or even years to come. At the end of the day it was a necessary business decision.

LESSONS:

Sometimes you face difficult tasks in business and it's best to take them head on and deal with them as early as possible. While it's important to build relationships with staff to get them working at their best and to really keep your fingers on the pulse, at same time you must keep a little distance. It's a delicate balance, but something you must strive to maintain.

It's also important for other employees to know that you will take action and discipline them if necessary and there are boundaries. They must have a clear understanding of what is expected of them, their responsibilities and the consequences of not meeting those responsibilities.

Employees who do not have boundaries and clearly defined responsibilities, will often push the boundaries, just as children do, and sometimes this can even result in outright employee fraud, with activities such as slacking off during the day and then claiming overtime to do the work outside of normal business hours.

The day you decide an employee is not right for your business must be the day you say goodbye to them.

We were going to learn this valuable lesson first-hand, closer to the moment of impact, as our business grew and we relied on others to manage their teams.

Continuous Improvement and the Quality Circle

Two concepts we implemented into our processes were 'continuous improvement' and 'quality circle'. Both concepts were developed right back in the 1950s by American mathematician, Dr Edwards Deming. These concepts were largely ignored by US industry, but were embraced by the Japanese, particularly in the automobile industry. They implemented them to improve the quality of their products and within 20 years, were dominating the market across the globe.

Deming's Quality Circle

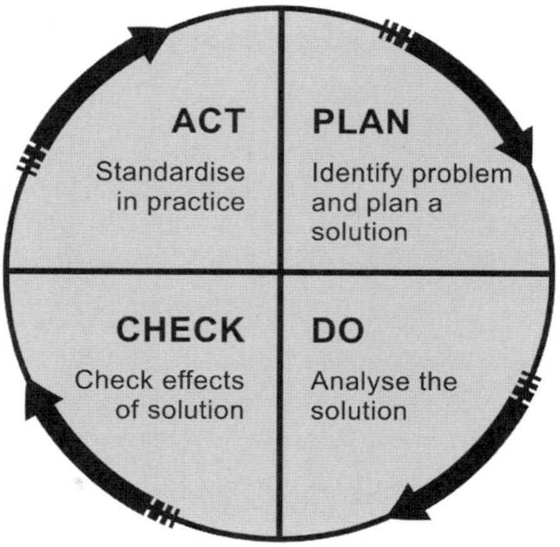

The basic principle is that you never rest on your laurels, but always look for ways of improving your processes and the quality of your products and services.

Everybody in the process should be made aware of how the part they play contributes to the overall product or service. They should be invited to suggest how their tasks or output could be improved and rewarded for making suggestions that result in improvement.

The Deming process ensures everybody in the organization is aligned with the goals of the organization.

My Notes / Thoughts

CHAPTER 8

More Vulnerable Than We Ever Imagined!

CHAPTER 8

More Vulnerable Than We Ever Imagined!

There's a golden rule in business when it comes to clients: never have one big client that you can't afford to lose. When one single client provides you with 25% of your business or more, and you lose that client, you could well be out of business.

In our case, it was more like 30%, and although that client was the principal buyer for a number of tree purchasers within their organization who had dealt with Paul faithfully for years, we realized it was really not a good situation to be in.

This client had been nurtured directly by Paul and although his expertise was part of the attraction, the long-term relationship was mainly due to the personal rapport he'd built with the main decision makers at the company.

Robert saw that and tried hard to keep that relationship going, but he could not seem to connect well with the management and they decided the following year to invite other suppliers to tender for their work.

This was a great opportunity for our competitors. They had never thought they would get a chance at this business, as Paul had locked them out for so long.

So the floodgates opened and they grasped the opportunity with both hands, quoting ridiculously low to get their foot in the door and ensure our monopoly with this client was lost forever.

We had failed to notice when we bought the business was that there was no binding contract with this client. They did not have to source their plants from our nursery, so, in effect, a large percentage of our sales were generated through a personal relationship that we were struggling to maintain.

We were devastated. We had not seen this coming and it had the ability to send us to the wall.

There was absolutely nothing we could do about it either; they were free to buy their stock from whoever they chose in the absence of any contract. They had been bending the rules for Paul and were obviously not going to continue it, now that he'd left.

Income slowed, production slowed, while we struggled to come to grips with this devastating change. How had this happened? Sure, Robert didn't click initially with them, but we went out of our way to do the best we could for this client. We always gave them the best stock we had. We kind of thought they'd stick with us anyway, rather than going to all the hassle of the tendering process, having to deal with new suppliers, and forge new relationships.

We began to wonder who would benefit from our demise. Was Ashley involved? We'd kept him on with generous incentives, but he'd rushed to a competitor the moment his contract expired and his bonus was paid.

He was very familiar with our client, he'd dealt with them on a number of occasions – and the company he'd moved to would certainly appreciate the business…

Then something much more sinister occurred to us

Paul had provided the vendor finance to us to purchase the business and this was a significant proportion of the purchase price about 40%. In retrospect, I believe that he thought we would falter at the first real obstacle and he would get the business back for nothing.

A vendor with few principles could have a huge windfall by engineering the downfall of someone in our position.

We did eventually recover from this major challenge and went on to repay every cent of the vendor finance, never once giving Paul cause for complaint. It was a massive relief when that imposition was removed from our shoulders but it may have unfortunately been a contributing factor to setting us on the path to the moment of impact. We began to let down our guard financially as we no longer had to watch every penny.

When you buy a business, especially one that is doing well, there are so many things you have to leave to trust. It would be nearly impossible to document everything. In hindsight, perhaps we could have requested Paul to produce a contract with this client – or failing that, we should have negotiated a price reduction based on the instability of some of the business, but as beginners in business, these things never crossed our minds.

So when we did the financial accounts at the end of the second year we were down a massive 22% on the last financial year, with serious cash-flow issues. We were devastated! This was despite bringing on new clients, without which it would have been a disaster.

Had it not been for Robert's financial background, we might have tried to continue trading and ultimately come to a sticky end, as many Australian businesses do. But Robert was pedantic about accounts and about not attempting to trade while insolvent, so he did the only ethical thing possible in our situation to save the company. He cashed in some of his superannuation. $150,000 to be exact.

We scraped through by the skin of our teeth. We had survived our second year – much poorer but much wiser. Determined to prove our doubters wrong and even knock them out of the way to become the dominant player in the industry!

We then took action to extend our range of clients so that not a single one accounted for more than 10–12% of total revenue.

LESSONS:

A big mistake many business owners make is to rest on their laurels after attracting a major client that accounts for a large percentage of their business. With major players now dominating many retail markets, this has become quite a common practice for farmers and smaller food producers and manufacturers. Unfortunately, it not only leaves them vulnerable to losing their business completely, it leaves them vulnerable to being squeezed by their major client, who may reduce prices to the point where the business becomes unprofitable.

In our situation, it was even worse because that major part of our business was not secured with a contract; it was built on a relationship and was entirely dependent on that relationship. It was really a shortcut to the moment of impact!

A good business coach should pick this up immediately, looking at your books and set you on a course of diversification. Creating new products or targeting new markets. This can be done by making a component of your business retail, if you are a wholesaler, or making the average sale larger for your other customers or clients. You can do this by finding a complimentary product or service that you can sell with your existing product or service.

The classic example of upselling is McDonald's getting their sales staff to ask: "Would you like fries and a coke with that" when people buy burgers. They increased the average sale and profits as their cost component was much lower on fries and soft drinks. Of course, over time they made that accepted by the market as the standard purchase, by packaging it into meals.

Diversification is critical for your long-term survival in business.

Another important lesson we learned was to never underestimate the importance of relationships. It's true that it's much easier for a client to stay with their existing supplier, especially if they are being looked after, but humans are emotional creatures. We often don't operate on logic or take the easiest path. When someone genuinely likes you, they are going to be much more likely to bend the rules or do what it takes to keep your business relationship going.

The more products you supply to a client, the more difficult it is for them to move. Look at the way banks get you to a have a bank account, credit cards, home loan, insurance, retirement fund etc. It makes it really difficult for you to transfer away from the bank even if they are costing you more in fees!

You should try and wrap up your clients in this manner, so that it is nearly impossible for them to find another supplier that does everything that you do.

Be very wary of any business you have, where you have not been able to forge a good relationship with your client or customer. It can easily be taken away by a competitor. Eighty percent of clients will leave you to purchase elsewhere because of perceived indifference! You must let your clients know you genuinely care for them. Most business owners think that price is the major reason why a customer leaves. After many surveys it has been noted that businesses have put price fifth on the list of reasons. The major reason being perceived indifference. It means that the supplier had taken the client for granted and assumed they would be loyal. In most instances regular contact with the client showing them you care would alleviate their decision to find an alternative supplier.

It is crucial to gain trust from your clients, prospects and suppliers. Trust is everything in a business. It maintains your client base, gains you new clients, provides you with referrals, and it can remove price out of the equation.

We built client relationships where they would place an order and not even bother to discuss the price. They did it this way because they trusted us and knew we would not take advantage of them and that we'd always provide them with good quality stock.

The Real Sales Process Begins After The Sale

1. **Acquisition** is the final step in the process of turning a lead into a customer or client, but as you can see from the diagram above, it is the first step in the sales process for businesses who want repeat sales and long-term stability.

2. **Retention** comes from ensuring the initial buying experience was good, the customer or client's questions were satisfactorily answered and they made an informed decision to buy rather than being pressured into a sale. They enjoyed the sales process and felt you cared about them and will buy again from you.

3. **Satisfaction** relates to their experience with your product or service. Is it everything it was made out to be? Does it exceed their expectations? Satisfaction will be at its highest if you under-promised and over-delivered – and there are some pleasant surprises for them – features they didn't expect, or quality that is beyond what they expected.

4. **Loyalty** comes from consistency. Their first great experience was not an isolated one – every time they buy, their experience is the same. The product or service is of a consistent high quality and customer support has been there whenever they needed it.

5. **Advocacy** should come naturally from a loyal customer, but perhaps you could help them to this stage with a referral

program – offering a discount or cash reward for referrals they bring into the business. Most people want to help friends or associates solve problems and if your product or service is the answer, they will happily recommend it.

Remember, a good recommendation is the cheapest customer or client to acquire – they convert quickly and easily and provided the experience is as they expected, they will quickly go on to become advocates.

By turning your customers or clients into advocates, you will reduce sales and marketing costs, increase profits and build a sustainable long-term business.

My Notes / Thoughts

CHAPTER 9

The Phone Call that Changed Everything

CHAPTER 9

The Phone Call that Changed Everything

Early one morning, Robert received a phone call.

It was an invitation to a free breakfast. Robert knew they were trying to sell something, that was pretty obvious. But he was nobody's fool and he felt like he needed an excuse to get out of the office for a while and away from this stress that had been building for the past few months.

If he'd really thought about it, Robert might have known he was right in 'the looking zone'– he was a hot prospect about to be sold and then go on to spend tens of thousands of dollars with this organization. But at this point, we were extremely naive when it came to marketing.

This simple phone call was really a turning point for us – it was the start of the next part of our journey and the start of a real roller coaster ride that was truly exhilarating – until the roller coaster collapsed at the moment of impact.

So Robert dressed in his smart business attire and drove off the following morning feeling very happy with himself – keen to tuck into a wholesome breakfast and show the sales people they'd picked the wrong guy.

This breakfast was truly magnificent – well worth the trip. It had been organised by an international business coaching organization as one of their main lead generators and they had mastered the art of getting people to sign up. So when Robert enjoyed their food, behaved attentively at the briefing, then masterfully escaped without signing anything. He never really got away scot-free.

That was all part of the sales process.

The follow up

The next day's follow up call was directly from James, the presenter at the breakfast. This guy was good. Robert reluctantly agreed to a meeting with him that very day in our office, still believing he had the power to resist.

The moment I caught sight of the black Porsche pulling into our car park however, I began to fear we were out of our league. James was dressed impeccably. He pulled on an expensive looking, perfectly pressed suit jacket, glanced at his gold Rolex and then confidently strode up to the office door.

A warm, firm handshake and we got straight down to business. It was true we didn't have a lot to be proud of after last financial year's debacle – in fact, we felt a little ashamed, that we'd been taken for a ride by the former owner, employees and a client – but we still kind of felt in control. We had a plan to address the cash-flow problems and recover – it was just a plan at this stage, but we seemed to be heading in the right direction. We felt like real Aussie battlers, determined to triumph against all odds!

But James didn't focus on our mistakes, he was complimentary. He applauded our determination and reflected on how quickly we were learning and adapting. But he cautioned us: these were not the only problems we were going to have and sometimes you work so hard in your business, you forget to work on the business. You just don't see the next problem until it hits you like a freight train – and then it's too late.

By the end of our meeting we probably would have bought anything James had recommended to us and we pretty well jumped at his offer of a business coach. It was true we could do with someone to 'third eye' our operations and turbocharge our recovery. The extra money we were going to make from this investment would more than cover the fees for the coach. We considered this as an investment, not an expense.

And so we were introduced to the concept of having a business coach. A good move, except for one small detail: we never thought to question the personal experience our coach had. We trusted James completely to assign us the right person with the right experience to handle our situation.

We were to find out further towards the moment of impact, that this was a fatal mistake.

There is an expression "You don't know what you don't know". In this case how true that was. Despite being involved with many businesses through the bank, Rob had never heard of a business coach let alone met one. So we had no idea what to expect but could see the value of having a separate person with knowledge in this area assisting us.

We have learnt that one of the most important things when in negotiations is what questions to ask, and how to ask the right questions.

LESSONS:

The first lesson we learned through our dealing with James and his organization, was the importance of the follow up in the sales process. Had James not followed up Robert, he would have missed that sale and the tens of thousands of dollars we spent with his organization over the next few years.

Studies on the sales process have shown that 80% or more of sales are made after the seventh contact, but 92% of sales people have given up by the fourth contact.

Continuing to follow up prospects that are lukewarm or guarded is difficult, particularly when you don't have a system, or have any of the process automated. Many small business owners who are new to sales take rejection personally and never really get around to asking that prospect again for the sale.

Having a sales system ensures they are religiously followed up and your return on investment is maximised for any marketing or advertising expenditure.

We usually advise and assist our clients to set up a CRM (client relationship management system) with some automated follow up options.

With the power of the internet many of the contacts with prospect can be automated through emails, buffering the business owner or sales staff from some of the rejection you get in the initial contacts – and ensuring the follow up process continues.

With the first contacts being emails or social media, phone calls only need to be made later in the process with prospects who are highly qualified. So the rate of rejection is much lower and the prospect is already familiar with you and your products or services.

The best tool I have seen for properly understanding the sales process is the Sales Pyramid, developed by the late marketing genius, Chet Holmes. It looks like this:

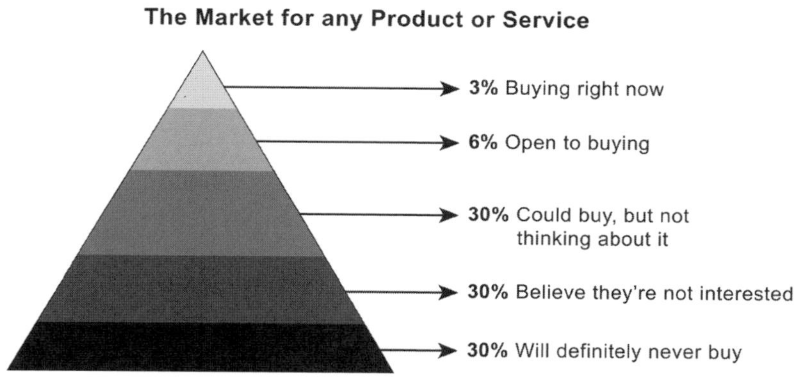

When you consider that only 3% of the market is ready to buy any potential product or service at any given time, you realize the importance of following up.

A business that does not follow up prospective clients or customers will only ever tap into 3% of the market. The 6% who are open to buying and the 30% who are not thinking about it, but could buy will be lost to competitors.

Obviously the 3% who are buying right now require very little follow up. They have their credit cards out and are ready to do the deal.

The 6%, who are open to buying however, are shopping around. They're comparing prices and more importantly, looking for somebody they can trust. If these prospects are diligently followed up, your efforts could result in a sale over the next couple of months.

If you don't follow them up, they will quite possibly have forgotten about you when they are ready to buy and will be looking at your competitors' products or services.

The 30% who could buy, but are not thinking about it will require even more follow up. Your goal with them should not be to push for a sale, but to educate and inform them. Send them valuable information that will eventually help them make a buying decision. The goal is to build rapport with them, and they see you as 'the industry expert' for them so that they naturally come to you when they are ready to buy.

By following up in this way, your business will have a steady stream of leads and sales, and you can potentially increase your sales tenfold.

My Notes / Thoughts

CHAPTER 10

Getting Clarity

CHAPTER 10

Getting Clarity

In the corporate world we came from, Robert and I had never really experienced business coaching or mentoring. All the training we received was relevant to our jobs. We never really received training on goal setting or attended any motivational seminars.

This was a whole new world for us and the more we tasted, the more we wanted. We'd really felt like we were under siege for a long time, fighting in the trenches, us against the world – or certainly the industry!

We'd started out with such a positive outlook, full of confidence, sharing our glorious vision with the staff wherever possible. And it was contagious. They had also caught it and really felt like they were part of something big. It was reflected in their work – they were productive and engaged.

But this positive outlook had been slowly declining, as we were confronted with one betrayal after another. Inwardly, we continued to be motivated and focused on our goals, but outwardly, people were noticing a difference. We'd become a little cynical and generally expected the worst outcome from every situation.

So one of the most important things we got from our coaching was new hope. The realisation that we had everything we needed to succeed. The wood was all stacked up; we just need a spark to make a raging bonfire.

This meant that Richard, the coach James allocated to us, walked into a very welcoming environment. Richard was young, perhaps to the point of betraying his lack of real-world experience, but that didn't matter to us at the time. James had sold us a dream. A dream that anything was possible... That we had the ability to achieve whatever we desired. We just needed that bit of a lift to get us going.

There is a wonderful definition of a coach that is: "someone who sees more in you than you see in yourself and helps you to bring it out." Despite his lack of hands on experience, Richard was certainly masterful at that.

He had the same air of confidence about him as James, dressed smartly and listened intently to what we had to say. He made us feel we were in control and we were headed in the right direction. He would occasionally interject with some suggestions that always made a lot of sense. He didn't refer much back to James or ask him questions, but that was something we didn't really notice at the time.

Our weekly session with Richard was something we truly looked forward to. It gave us clarity and reassurance that we were on the right path and everything was going to work out. Most importantly, we'd reclaimed back our passion. We expected the best outcome from every situation and started to get it.

This started to rub off on our staff and you could really see the difference in their attitude and more importantly, their level of engagement. Their jobs began to be more meaningful and they again began to feel they were part of something worthwhile.

LESSONS:

The experience of engaging a coach taught us that it doesn't matter what the circumstances, things won't really begin to happen until you really have the passion and clearly defined goals and direction.

Having a positive attitude is infectious. It rubs off on your staff and ensures they have a higher level of engagement, which in turn increases productivity, improves customer service, and ultimately your bottom line.

Having a coach gave us someone to speak with and bounce ideas off. It removed that feeling of isolation. We have spoken to many business owners and they all say the same thing, "It's a very lonely occupation being the 'Boss of a business' as you are on your own in almost everything. You can't ask your staff as they don't care about your issues and think that if you run a business you must be a millionaire! You often can't even ask your spouse or family, so having someone that understands is a great benefit."

There are a growing number of businesses world-wide who see the benefits of having a coach. According to the International Coaching Federation (ICF) in their 2016 report, the coaching industry is a $2.3 billion dollar industry worldwide and it grew by 19% in the five years from 2011–2016.

The reason is simple: it works. This is why every top athlete in international competition has a coach and why it has become the norm for executives in large companies. They often don't get good feedback on their performance from their peers or subordinates and need somebody who is not afraid to 'tell it like it is', to help them grow.

In small business a good coach can be even more effective, as we are usually so busy working in the business, we neglect to work on the business. Here are some of the benefits of engaging a business coach:

1. They will give you 'short-cuts' or 'cheats' to success. When you have a coach, you no longer have to learn everything by trial and error – your coach should have either experienced the situation themselves or seen other people experience it and be able to give you the solution. Your coach can give you the tools and the tricks that they've found to be successful.

2. As an outside voice or 'third eye' a business coach brings an outside perspective to the table. You can sound your ideas with them, to get help comparing and deciding which idea will work best. It saves you rolling out ideas that are doomed to fail.

3. We all hit a brick wall at some stage in our business – we get bogged down so deep, we can't step back and look at the bigger picture. There is usually a very simple solution for what seems to be an overwhelming problem and a business coach will help you find that solution.

   We can become stagnant in our business, just going through the motions and treading water, unable to break out and move to the next level. A good business coach will help us see where we are and help us continue to grow our business.

4. Many business owners get stuck in their comfort zone, unable or unwilling to try new things, new ways of marketing or bringing in business. If we don't move out of this comfort zone, we can eventually lose our clients or customers to more aggressive and innovative competitors. So your coach will help you and motivate you to try new things – to get out and meet people, to try marketing methods nobody else in your industry is using.

5. A good coach will also take the time to become familiar with your business – to learn it inside and out. They will immediately see things that don't seem right – things that have probably escaped your attention because you're too close to them. They can help you head off pending disasters before they occur.

   For instance, a coach may notice something odd about the behaviour of a staff member, that uncovers a high level of employee fraud, or notice inefficiencies in the way they operate and help you to streamline the process, saving money and improving service.

6. Paying for a coach will force you to focus on developing your business during these sessions. The coach and business owner usually develop a synergy and ideas start flowing. You will find yourself coming up with brilliant ideas for your business that you never would have even thought about without your coach.

   This will also give you self-confidence and certainty. You'll forget the bruises you gained from battling in the business and rise up to try and achieve new things. Just having someone in your corner, cheering for you can make a massive difference.

7. Even though you are taking time off your normal work to meet with your coach and to implement changes in your business, you'll begin to see increased productivity. This is because your coach will maximise your potential and that of your key staff members.

   As you begin to systematize your business, you'll make their job easier and more rewarding and you'll see an increase in engagement and productivity from your staff. As this increases, you'll find that you have to spend less and less time in the business – in fact, you may well find that the business begins to run better when you're not around!

8. Finally, your business coach will help you make more money! The end result of everything you do with your coach will be an increase in your profits. You'll work together to streamline systems, to reach out to more potential customers and clients, to improve your employee engagement and their level of service. This all has a way of increasing income and reducing costs.

Although our own coaching experience was good, we still had some valuable lessons to learn about engaging a business coach and choosing the right person. While we enjoyed all these benefits early in our coaching, there were certain things our coach neglected to advise us on, simply because he didn't have the experience of growing a business to the size we were growing to.

This was unfortunately a Lesson we would not learn until just before the moment of impact…

My Notes / Thoughts

CHAPTER 11

Follow Your Heart

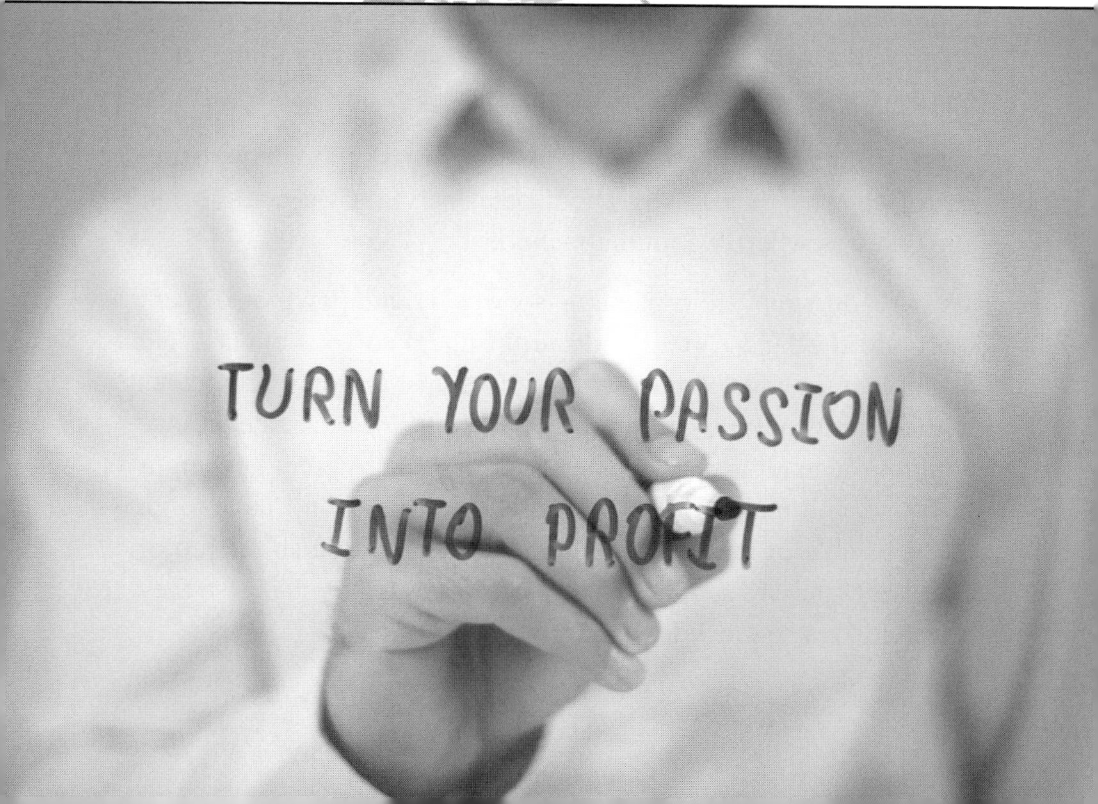
TURN YOUR PASSION
INTO PROFIT

CHAPTER 11

Follow Your Heart

We still had this major problem hanging over our heads – that was the seasonal nature of the business. It was completely alien to us and took exceptional money management skills, especially after relying on a steady wage for most of our working life.

We had borrowed heavily to buy the business and then had to prop up our losses with Robert's superannuation, so it was almost impossible for us to take another overdraft to get us through those off-season months.

What we needed was a counter-cyclical business which was busy when our core business was flat.

We thought long and hard about how we could extend our business, to generate an income to cover the quiet times. We thought about other markets further afield, about perhaps expanding to the retail market where we imagined customers came in all year.

We thought about how we could upsell or cross sell to our existing customers and then finally about other services we could offer, and that was where we hit the Jackpot!

We already supply the plants – so why couldn't we also plant them, do the landscaping and nurture them for our clients? No one at that time was doing anything like this. It would provide us with a significant increase in the profitability of each sale and we could provide all the services that our clients required, keeping it in-house, and making it easy for them, so they didn't have to go to the trouble of bringing in other contractors to finish the job. It also meant that we supplied multiple services to our clients so they were unlikely to move to our competitors.

Just by chance, every day on our way to work we'd drive past a new housing subdivision that was being built. It was huge and we'd talk about the number of trees they would need and wonder who would be supplying those trees.

It then occurred to us we'd missed something right in front of our noses: here was our chance to kick off our new landscaping business, right in our local area!

We discussed this with Richard, our business coach at the weekly meeting – though I knew what he would say. Of course he thought it was a fantastic idea that we should pursue with all the energy and enthusiasm we could muster.

So early one morning on my way to work, I drove into the site and headed to the new subdivision office. I was warmly met by the resident sales executive whose smile quickly faded once she learned I was not a potential buyer, but her interest didn't. We spoke for a while and I explained who we were and what services we could provide. She committed to speak with the owner, which she did, but they didn't get back to me right away.

A week went by, then another, while each day we'd drive past the subdivision and see no planting activity at all. "They'll have to do something sooner or later," I told Robert. "It was worth a try…" he replied reassuringly. "Of course, they have their own contracts, probably long-term suppliers." So I followed up, calling in again. The sales executive assured me she had spoken to the developer, but still another couple of weeks went by with no contact.

Disappointed, I resigned myself to the reality that it had been a long shot and perhaps it would never come to fruition. I thought about approaching other developers, and how it would be worth our while planning out a constructive approach and defining who we actually would want to target. There were obviously established players looking after that market and it would be challenging for an outsider to break in, but we were prepared to take that risk and go for it!

It was about that time, when I was contemplating the challenges of this new market, when my phone rang.

"You called by our office weeks ago to talk about providing us with landscaping." My jaw dropped. "The owner would like to set a time to meet with you." Here I was having this telephone conversation and at the same time waving my hands in the air trying to get everyone's attention. This was our big break!

In an incredible twist, their regular landscape provider had let them down. He'd taken their business for granted and dropped the ball. We now had literally the opportunity of a lifetime. If we worked hard and impressed this client, we were in.

We could easily use their recommendation to expand our services to other developers.

Best of all, our seasonal problems were about to be resolved. Our landscaping services would provide us with cash flow during the quiet season at the nursery.

There was a lot of work to be done and if we didn't quote the job properly, we'd either lose it for being overpriced or even worse, underquote it and lose money on it. But thankfully Robert was very good with numbers and he was able to properly assess everything that would be needed for the job, including the hours of labour. Our quote came in at a similar price they'd been quoted from their last supplier, so we were immediately accepted.

On the back of this success, I decided my time would be much better spent marketing our services, than doing what I really didn't like and struggled with day after day – the bookkeeping. A good bookkeeper was not that expensive to hire and would do the job much faster and more effectively than I could ever manage to.

So we advertised to find a good bookkeeper who understood the importance of maintaining cash flow, by ensuring invoices went out on time and suppliers were not paid ahead of time.

This was a turning point in our business and the point when I actually began to enjoy what I was doing. And I was good at it. Up to that point in my life I had never known what I really wanted to do. Yes I had great jobs and was good at them, but they were never passion jobs!

Once I found my purpose, there was no stopping me. My passion more than made up for my lack of industry knowledge and I found I could confidently and convincingly approach and liaise with potential clients.

LESSONS

The main lesson we learned from this experience was to never discount any potential business. You never know when somebody is going to drop the ball and give you that opening you need to expand into a whole new market.

By getting that first client and looking after them so well that they become a raving fan, it is not difficult to do.

You also have to think about how you can expand your business by adding a complementary service or by adding products or services that relate to your core business.

The easiest people to sell to are your existing clients or customers and eventually we were able to sell our landscaping services to our existing nursery clients.

The cheapest marketing you will ever do and that with the highest return on investment, is marketing to your existing clients and customers.

Another lesson we learned is that our time is extremely important. We should always maximise our efficiency by taking on tasks we are good at and delegating those we are not good at, to somebody who can do them more effectively. In most small family businesses, the wife manages the books by default – it's a tradition we seem to have. But often, as in our case, our time is much better spent promoting your business to potential clients or customers.

Bookkeeping too is a specialised field. A good bookkeeper will literally keep your business afloat, collecting invoice payments on time and ensuring suppliers are not paid earlier than necessary. They will also ensure tax payments are all up-to-date, to avoid paying interest and penalties.

Maintaining good cash-flow is extremely important for business survival. The majority of small businesses that fail in Australia do so because of cash-flow problems. According to the Australian Bureau of Statistics, 30% of Australian small businesses have failed since 2008 and the leading cause of failure (at 68%) is Poor Cash Flow.

These business owners were probably good at what they did and in many cases had all the business they needed to succeed – they just couldn't keep the cash flowing to stay afloat.

You don't want to toil hard and risk all your money just to become another statistic. A good bookkeeper is essential for any successful business.

Here are some real benefits of hiring a professional bookkeeper:

1. They will help you minimise or eliminate potentially costly mistakes. There are a multitude of mistakes that can be made with bookkeeping and they can have serious consequences on your cash flow and even threaten your survival.

When staff or business owners do the books on a part-time basis, on top of their other duties, they are prone to make far more mistakes than a professional bookkeeper who does this all the time.

2. A good bookkeeper will help you save money by paying bills promptly, eliminating late fees, penalties and interest. You will also save time by not having to deal with suppliers who are calling to chase up accounts and will have the peace of mind, knowing your tax obligations are all up-to-date.

3. You'll get paid quicker. When you're doing a multitude of tasks, it's easy to forget things like issuing an invoice on time or following up invoices. A good bookkeeper will wherever possible automate this system, ensuring you are paid on time. Your bookkeeper may also ensure that your terms of invoicing are included in any contracts or tender documents so that you set up an agreement with clients or customers on the timeframe for payment.

4. You'll free up your own time to do more productive things. You'll probably find that you can use this time to bring in much more money than you pay your bookkeeper. Your bookkeeper will do the tasks much more quickly and efficiently that you will and will possibly utilise professional software to make it even quicker.

   You'll probably find that engaging a bookkeeper ends up costing you nothing and you even gain money from it.

5. You'll gain a better understanding of your business, which may change the way you quote jobs or the way you manage staff. Having regular profit-and-loss statements helps you identify irregularities and take action to prevent any real losses.

It will also help you identify employee fraud and theft and nip it in the bud before it becomes a major issue.

It also gives you a regular health check, so that you can be sure that what you're doing is profitable and sustainable. It will allow you to regularly fine tune your business to continue to grow.

As you generally only pay for the time you need, hiring a bookkeeper is usually cost effective, even for small businesses. As you grow and your accounts become more complex, you can increase the time you need them for. It gives you an affordable, scalable solution that really can pay dividends.

My Notes / Thoughts

CHAPTER 12

Let's Try That Again

CHAPTER 12

Let's Try That Again

Now that we'd successfully managed to diversify and were on the way to having a much more predictable, regular income, we decided to go back and build up the nursery again, as it was still struggling after the loss of that major client.

What was even worse was that company we'd lost was capitalising on the desperation they'd forced upon us. They'd call us in at the last minute, for jobs they couldn't tender or jobs their new suppliers had screwed up. They were basically using us as their backup plan. It was a very demeaning and uncomfortable situation to be in. We had to do something about it.

We identified local government authorities as a predictable lucrative area for our business growth. The major client we'd lost was supplying to them, so we decided take them on and supply directly to them, cutting out the middle man.

We did some research.

To secure contracts with local government authorities, of course, you had to first wait for them to call for tenders and then compete with other businesses for the contract.

Although we were newbies in the nursery business, we had a huge advantage over our competition: coming from corporate backgrounds and preparing reports was second nature to us and a tender is very similar in many ways. We did some research and found out what local government authorities looked for in a tender, what they expected to see and we made it as simple as possible for them.

Compliance was a big one – Occupational Health and Safety (OH&S) – and believe it or not, Paul was not up to scratch with this, despite having some long term local government clients. We bit the bullet and brought in a consultant, spending money we couldn't really spare, but we knew it was critical to build a bigger customer base so the business was more secure.

Now OH&S is a bigger issue in this country than many small business owners realize. Owners and managers who neglect to act on safety issues, or run organizations that are not compliant with safety regulations, can be held personally liable for deaths or injuries that result from that negligence. And the penalties are severe – personal fines can run into hundreds of thousands of dollars and there are jail terms for more serious offenders.

As with other areas of law, ignorance is no defence – so it is something you must get on top of, especially if your business has a workshop, factory or outdoor component, where employees are using machinery or motor vehicles.

OH&S was not something we were really aware of when we were assessing different businesses and we did not look very closely at it when we bought this one. But in hindsight, we should have been able to insist that it was all brought up to scratch and properly documented before the handover, saving us precious time and money.

We set about the task of ensuring we were fully compliant and had all the necessary documentation that a local government body would require. This was no mean feat because we recognised the need to have everything documented.

We then took it a step further and obtained accreditation in this area, so each year we would be audited to maintain our accreditation. Once we'd achieved this, we began to tender for local government contracts and started to win them.

We had at least reached a milestone in our new life adventure. Finally we'd gone past just holding things together. We were expanding – building a wonderful future for ourselves and silencing our critics.

Even our staff started looking at us with more respect.

Rob's most satisfying moment to that point was when he was constantly being asked his advice on tree selection by qualified arborists. This really was full circle in the learning and knowledge area.

There was no stopping us from this point.

LESSONS:

OH&S compliance is a big deal and it's not something you normally look at when evaluating a business. Most businesses are compliant to some degree, but where there are gaps in compliance, there is a chance of someone being killed or injured and you as the business owner being held personally accountable for it.

Penalties for non-compliance which exposes workers to accidents or illness vary from state to state in Australia. Maximum fines for corporations are generally over one million dollars, with fines for individuals running into hundreds of thousands of dollars with the possibility of imprisonment.

The act makes occupational health and safety everybody's responsibility. Basically, staff should all know their health and safety obligations and receive regular training in health and safety that applies to their job.

There should be open and honest communication across the organization, with staff being able to report safety hazards or near-misses and management taking action to ensure changes are made to make the workplace safer.

If there is a culture of recklessness and risk-taking in your company, it must be changed and people who break the rules or condone rule breaking by others must be held accountable.

Compliance involves having necessary safety equipment wherever there is a workplace risk and ensuring that safety equipment is properly maintained and the maintenance is documented. It also involves having safety officers and ensuring staff receive necessary safety training relevant to their work.

Fire prevention is also a part of your safety plan and along with having a fire warden and fire safety equipment, your staff must be trained in the correct procedures to take in case of a fire. Regular fire drills also need to be conducted.

As our nursery was based in a rural area, snakes would sometimes come in for the water during dry months. So our OH&S also had to include a plan on the action staff should take when they discovered a snake and treatment to be given in the event of a snake bite.

OH&S is really a necessity. Before this legislation was introduced in western countries, the cost of industrial accidents was immense. Statistics show that during the Vietnam War era, more Americans were killed at home through Industrial accidents than died fighting in Vietnam.

The Australian statistics were equally shocking.

Neglecting OH&S will accelerate you to the moment of impact.

Proper documentation is essential for tendering, particularly with government contracts and when OH&S has been neglected, it can be a costly exercise to correct it. When buying a business, one of the requirements should be an independent OH&S audit, conducted by a qualified expert.

The benefits of staying on top of OH&S cannot be overstated. An unsafe, hazardous workplace has a detrimental effect on the morale of your employees. It will result in a lack of regard for the organization, employee disengagement, low productivity and employee fraud.

By being fully OH&S compliant and engaging employees in that process, they will feel much better about you and your organization, be more engaged, more productive and you will attract better quality applicants to fill vacancies.

And that translates to higher profits. A study of the American workplace by Gallup in 2013 found that companies with higher employee engagement had profit margins 22% higher than companies with low engagement. They were 21% more productive and had 48% fewer safety incidents.

So even the process of engaging employees in safety awareness reduces the number of accidents in your workplace and increases your profit margin.

My Notes / Thoughts

CHAPTER 13

A Big Dose of Motivation

CHAPTER 13

A Big Dose of Motivation

Richard's coaching organization was a big one and regular seminars were held in Melbourne. It provided good business information and the more we got the more we craved. It was infectious. After a few short months, we found ourselves bound for Las Vegas, to see the international head of the organization speak at a three-day seminar.

We couldn't afford it, we were coming out of a disastrous year and although things had just started moving upwards we weren't flush with cash, so we got out our credit cards and booked the trip. Richard encouraged us, and even Robert, who is very analytical by nature, thought the benefits would outweigh the costs.

It was an intensive, high-level crash course in business, covering business success training and wealth creation and there was plenty there for both of us to absorb. Robert found good step-by-step methodology that he could immediately begin to apply, while I found ways to stay ahead of the game so I could bring in more business. We mixed with like-minded people from all over the world and the energy was infectious.

For five wonderful days, we enjoyed the most luxurious surroundings and five-star service. It really gave us a taste of what our life could be like if we succeeded. Both of us came away invigorated, our batteries charged and extremely confident we could achieve whatever we set our mind to.

That trip to Vegas truly put us on a whole new level. Richard's coaching had changed our whole outlook, but this was something else again. Things really started to happen for us once we returned from Vegas!

We were on fire! Our staff really noticed the difference. Robert moved around with an air of authority. He was an expert working in his field of expertise. For me it was motivational and I saw so many possibilities open up before me. I put together a vision board with images of things I wanted to achieve, both in business and in life. I pasted an image of a Bentley, a motor boat, our ideal home and business headquarters. And images of the ideal lifestyle we wanted to live.

I could never have imagined doing this before the Vegas trip, but I hung my vision board on the office wall, right where it would constantly remind me of 'why' I had left my sheltered corporate life, risked everything and continued to work long hours, day after day.

Visitors to my office would comment on the board and ask me its purpose and I would proudly tell them, "That is what I will achieve."

The enthusiasm flowed into my work. I was unstoppable when bringing on new clients, they just knew when talking with me that our company was the best supplier they could possibly find. The 'right fit' for them. Our conversion rate went through the roof.

LESSONS:

This reinforced the power of motivation. Never underestimate what a motivated person can achieve – it is really the secret ingredient for success. But motivation without activities to channel it into is worthless – it soon dissipates without something to focus it on.

We were extremely worried about maxing out our credit cards to go to Las Vegas, we took a leap of faith, but the trip proved to be so valuable, we made our money back a hundred-fold.

It taught us the value of seminars – but not motivational seminars alone. A seminar which provides you with both the motivation and the tools to immediately start to use and to channel that motivation into gold.

Running a small business can be the loneliest place in the world and without training and motivation you can slowly lose your enthusiasm and slip down to the moment of impact.

Remember that famous quote from President Lincoln – *"Give me six hours to chop down a tree and I will spend the first four sharpening the axe"?* 'Sharpening the axe' or 'sharpening the saw' have become synonymous with training and motivation and education.

In his book *7 Habits of Highly Effective People*, the late Dr Steven Covey dedicated a full chapter to this, titled 'Sharpening the Saw'. It's basically about self-renewal and self-improvement. This is really foundational to everything else you will do in your business that leads to success.

But 'Sharpening the Saw' is not just about improving our business knowledge, it's about working on ourselves in four different and very important dimensions: Physical, Spiritual, Mental and Social/Emotional. Dr Covey says: *"It means exercising all four dimensions of our nature, regularly and consistently in a wise and balanced way."*

'Sharpening the Saw' is an ongoing process of personal change in all four dimensions:

1. The physical dimension means regularly exercising and maintaining a healthy body – this in turn gives us the energy we need to be able to effectively work both in our business and on our business. It also reduces stress and the damage that can do to our long-term health.

2. Working on your spiritual dimension could be any one of a number of activities depending on your belief system or your faith – it could be anything from spending time with your Church, Synagogue, Temple or Mosque community to just taking a walk in nature or meditating. It is recognition that we are more than just three-dimensional beings and there is another side to us which, if invigorated, will make us feel complete and happy.

3. Our mental dimension requires learning, training and motivation. If we continually challenge ourselves and exercise our mind, we will think in new and innovative ways. Seminars, training camps and events are great for sharpening the saw in the mental dimension. Training that we do in TAFE or university at night is also good for this.

4. The social/emotional dimension requires us to spend time with the people we love and doing the things we love – working on our relationships with our partners, children and family, so they don't fall apart through neglect. When you see somebody who is going through a relationship crisis trying to manage their tasks at work, it really brings home how important this is.

'Sharpening the Saw' must be balanced across these four 'dimensions'... or you will create an imbalance which you can offset for a while, but it will come back to bite you, long-term.

When you spend time regularly developing in all these four dimensions, you will be balanced, energetic, invigorated and full of optimism.

You can never undo what you learn – it's something nobody can take from you and you quickly discover what you don't know!

You feel like a frog that has lived his whole life in a small pond and knows everything about that pond, suddenly discovering that it is actually part of a much bigger pond he knows nothing about.

The more you learn, the more you find there is to learn and so it's an ongoing process that never really ends. And you don't want it to, anyway – It's a wonderful journey, full of excitement and discovery!

My Notes / Thoughts

CHAPTER 14

An Incredible Year

CHAPTER 14

An Incredible Year

Robert popped the bottle and the champagne started to flow. It was the first of many we'd consume that evening. We'd done it. Against the odds and with the rest of the industry against us, we'd succeeded!

It was the end of our third financial year in business. The first had been consistent with the last owner's income so we settled in quite well. The second year, however, had been a disaster when we lost most of the business from our one major client. The more we thought about it, the more likely it seemed that we'd been white-anted by the previous owner and our former manager. We'd come close to failing and only survived by cashing in some of Robert's superannuation.

But now, with the help of our business coach, we'd increased revenue by 65% in one year and not only that, our profit margin was also up. We had silenced the doubters! We'd beaten our adversaries! With no industry experience at all, no business experience, mortgaged to the hilt and beaten down, we'd come back and triumphed. We were on a roll and we were going to continue expanding until we dominated the industry in Melbourne.

The more we analysed our business, the better it looked.

We'd kept our overheads down. We still had our office in the tin shed we'd started out in and had resisted any temptations to move in to better premises.

We'd diversified – we now had a landscaping division as well as the nursery. They both made a healthy profit. We had survived Ashley's resignation and now had a much better replacement.

We'd trebled our staff from the initial five we'd inherited when we bought the business to over 15 and only one of the original employees remained. As they'd left, we'd replaced each one with a better qualified person, with a better attitude. The best part was that none of these people had any connection to the previous owner. They were all our people, loyal to us – the episode with Ashley leaving taught us to nurture relationships with staff, to never take their loyalty for granted.

Our new bookkeeper kept money coming in on time and ensured everybody was paid properly and we were fully compliant with tax.

Although the average wage we paid had increased, these people were more productive and engaged, so our profits were higher. And we had good cash flow, money coming in most of the time.

Best of all, or average sale per tree had gone from $80 to $300. Our business really looked like a textbook case of how to succeed and turn a failing business into a profit machine!

The happiest guy in the room seemed to be Richard. I guess he really felt a sense of accomplishment – and I imagine James was very happy with his performance. I bet they were showcasing our business as a shining example of the difference a good business coach would make.

Anybody listening in to our celebration would have thought they were listening to Napoleon's generals discussing their victories. We were invincible and we were going to conquer the world!

LESSONS

Our experience to date taught us the importance of staying the course – not giving up when we were faced with challenges that at times seemed insurmountable!

It reminds me of Napoleon Hill's story about the Darby's and the gold mine.

The Darby's were caught up in the gold fever in the US early last century, and went west to stake a claim and find their fortune. They went to work with pick and shovel, working long, hard days with their dreams of riches motivating them through the trials.

After weeks of hard toil, they finally struck traces of gold, but needed machinery to bring the ore to the surface. So they quietly covered up the mine and went home to raise the money from friends and relatives. They were all very excited about being part of a successful gold mining prospect, so they willingly invested in the venture. The machinery was bought and shipped back to the mine where they went to work.

The first car of ore they sent to a smelter had a very high gold content. In fact, they appeared to be sitting on one of the richest mines in Colorado! They would quickly clear any debts they had. But then came their big challenge: The vein of gold ore disappeared! They were at the end of their rainbow, and the pot of gold was missing!

They worked on, day after day, desperately trying to find the vein – but all efforts failed.

Despondent, they walked away. The machinery was sold for a few hundred dollars to a junk buyer and the Darby's took the train back home.

The junk man was no fool. He decided to get the advice of an expert before dismantling the machinery, so he called in a mining engineer. The engineer inspected the mine and advised him that the Darby's had probably been digging in the wrong direction to pick up the vein as they were not familiar with 'fault lines'.

The engineer estimated the vein would probably start again just three feet from where the Darby's had stopped digging! And that is exactly where it was found!

The Darby's gave up just three feet from discovering one of the richest gold mines in the country.

And so it is with business. When you reach your darkest hour, you are often very close to breaking through and succeeding. Don't be discouraged by challenges. Meet them head on and you will ultimately succeed.

My Notes / Thoughts

CHAPTER 15

Building The Empire

CHAPTER 15

Building The Empire

On the back of our new level of motivation and the recent business success we'd enjoyed, it was time to knuckle down and really get our business structured for expansion. At our weekly coaching session, we identified a key player we'd need to facilitate this: a highly qualified landscaping manager.

To date the people we'd hired for this role had been improving. Each time one left, we'd find somebody more experienced to replace them, but we had not managed to find a candidate who had the experience to act as a stand-alone manager.

Rob had previously quoted all the jobs and managed them from the office and we'd always employed a landscaper who had some experience of running a project but never had the credentials to take the business to next level and beyond.

This had worked well and we always made a profit on every job. But we knew that we needed a specific level of expertise if we were to take the business to the next level. We had been slowly increasing the value of the projects we undertook and due to Lorraine's persistence and marketing skills we had the opportunity to quote the largest project we had ever considered – $500,000. We met with the client and actually won the quote. At this point Robert realized this was probably beyond his area of expertise due to the level of complexity and size.

So this time, we decided to take it to the next level. We had a number of applications but one person's resume really looked perfect and ticked every box. When we called him in for an interview,

Shannon was comfortable and confident. He was a likeable guy and he'd previously held the position of general manager in other landscaping businesses. He'd previously owned his own business and had participated on Industry Boards.

We'd learned to use the DISC system for personality profiling at one of the seminars we attended and we found it invaluable for profiling applicants to see if they were a good fit for both their role and their team. While it was just one of many criteria we used, we found it very helpful.

Using DISC, we'd built teams within our organization that worked well together and were very engaged. The synergy was electric and they noticeably outperformed previous teams we'd had in the company.

Using DISC profiling, we found that Shannon was predominantly a high 'I' which meant he was outgoing and people oriented. He was inspirational and would certainly motivate a team to work well, we just hoped he was detail oriented enough to manage his projects tightly.

As landscaping manager, Shannon would free up Robert to concentrate on our core business – the nursery with our nursery manager, ensuring that neither business was neglected.

I was certain from what I'd seen with the local developers, there were some real opportunities for a good operator to take a lot of the business and I was very confident I could get many more to try our services. Meanwhile, there were plenty of opportunities to win local government authority tenders for the nursery.

Robert could easily outdo all our competitors when it came to putting together tender documents. And we maintained such a high level of quality; our existing clients were becoming raving fans and would happily sing our praises.

Shannon proved to be more ambitious than we ever imagined. He believed we shouldn't stop at housing subdivisions, but should take on other large commercial projects like hospitals, schools and shopping centres.

We loved the idea and talked it over with him on a number of occasions and also with Richard, our business coach. He encouraged us to go for it. It was going to be a hard market to break into though. There were already a number of well-established players servicing that market. We needed to get some contracts in that market.

Then Shannon came up with a real brainwave. "Let's hire someone who already has those contacts," he said. A Business Development Manager. Someone who can go out and find new projects and even new markets. Someone who can quote the projects, leaving Shannon free to manage his operation.

Now we were really on our way to building an empire!

LESSONS

The DISC system of personality profiling is a very credible methodology. It is a modern adaption of the four temperaments system which was developed by the Greek physician Hippocrates almost 2,500 years ago.

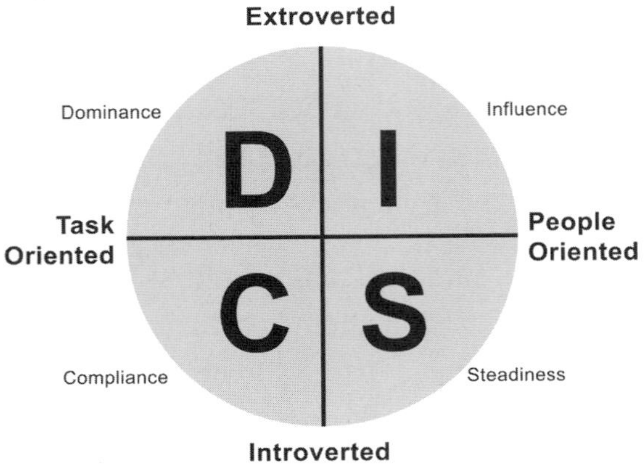

This is how it works

There are four basic personality types and most people will be strong in one, but will also have traits from at least two others. Very few people will fit into exactly into one personality type.

The more outgoing, driven people are usually high in the 'D' quadrant while entertainers and influencers are high in the 'I' quadrant. People who love detail and are happy to work away in the background, like accountants and engineers are usually high in the 'C' quadrant, while those who are very supportive, like teachers and nurses will be high in the 'S' quadrant.

By understanding what personality type staff are high in, you can understand what motivates them and the kind of environment they thrive in. For instance:

'D' personality types like to be in charge. They are usually problem solvers who want to push through and get things done. They can be unstoppable and sometimes quite arrogant. With 'D' types, it's usually 'My Way or the Highway'. They hate it when things are moving slowly or things are delayed because of red tape and will usually find a way to break through and get things done.

Corporate and political leaders are usually high 'D' type people.

'I' personality types on the other hand, crave popularity. They enjoy attention and can be funny and inspiring. They are usually the life of the party and can be very influential. They like people and enjoy being around them. Their biggest fear is disapproval of their friends or peers.

Actors and entertainers are usually high in this quadrant.

A person who is a combination of both 'D' and 'I' quadrants can be an extremely effective leader. Someone who is both driven and influential.

'S' personality types are usually somewhat shy and reserved. They work well with high 'D' and 'I' types because they are quite happy to have somebody else take the limelight and they are understanding and supportive. They are loyal and love everything to be consistent and orderly.

Interestingly some of the best corporate leaders in the world are actually high 'S' personality types. They are not leaders you ever read about in the news, because they shun publicity and don't like taking credit for their success – but they build successful and enduring organizations.

In the book *Good to Great*, about the most successful public companies in the US, author Jim Collins noticed a common trait with the leaders – they were all predominantly high 'S' type personalities. Leaders who put the longevity of their company before themselves and who always mentored a successor and supported them to be a better leader than they themselves were.

'C' type personalities are essential people to have on your team. They will study the detail in anything they do and pick up mistakes. They will read every word in the contract and analyze it. Every team should have at least one high 'C' type to ensure everybody else stays on track and does things properly. They thrive in an orderly, compliant atmosphere and hate disarray.

A bookkeeper who is a high 'C' personality will be gold to your business. They will not miss a thing.

Using DISC to profile potential clients and customers

When you understand the DISC system properly and can pick the dominant personality type in a prospect, you will be much more effective in presenting to them and following up with them.

For instance, if you were giving a presentation to someone who was a high 'I', you would not go into a lot of detail. Their eyes would glaze over and you would lose them. You would be more effective keeping the presentation exciting and interacting with them all the way through it. They love surprises and would not mind at all if you followed up out of the blue. Be careful though, they may keep you on the phone for a long period, wasting your time.

A high 'D' type will also not appreciate a lot of detail. They would want you to get to the point as quickly as possible, so they can go and do other tasks they have set for themselves. Their favourite saying is "What's the bottom line?" A high 'D' is probably the hardest person to present to. You should have a well-practised 'elevator pitch' ready for them – be able to effectively describe your business in three minutes and be able to quickly articulate what is in it for them and the process of getting started.

Always be straight to the point when following up, as they hate time-wasters and will be very intolerant of chit-chat.

Presenting to a high 'C' is being completely different. They will want to see all the details or specifications and will not be impressed if you didn't have them, or you didn't understand them. They will cross-examine you on everything and not miss a single detail. Plans and specification sheets are effective with high 'C's.

When you follow up with a high 'C' make sure you do it on schedule and have further information on hand, so you can effectively answer their questions.

A high 'S' is much more receptive when they feel you appreciate them and truly care that your product or service is going to be right for them.

They like consistency and are very uncomfortable with sudden change, so it is very important you keep any promises you make and follow up consistently.

People of this personality type can be incredible long-term clients or customers as they are intensely loyal.

So why understanding personality traits and DISC is so important for your business and understanding which people are right for which roles? By understanding the personal characteristics that are ideal for a particular role you can structure your recruitment procedures to appeal to people with the desired personality traits that suit the job.

This serves two purposes:

1. You get someone who has the right traits for the job; and
2. You employ someone who is doing something they really want to do and therefore a happy and contented employee.

A total win–win situation is formed.

My Notes / Thoughts

CHAPTER 16

The Deal of a Lifetime

CHAPTER 16

The Deal of a Lifetime

Shannon had been working out well and the landscaping business was thriving. We were all crowded into our original office, so it was time to get a new location.

Robert had let Shannon run the landscaping operation himself, with the occasional monitoring and assistance with quoting, and he was very happy with Shannon's progress. We believed he could now run the business alone from another location.

However, given what had happened in the past with staff like Ashley, we worried about our ability to keep someone like Shannon for the long term.

So after a few months it was suggested to Robert that we come up with an incentive deal and made Shannon a non-executive director of the newly established landscaping business. This would give Shannon perceived status in the business without any liability, and the incentive to work extra hard to make it succeed. Richard thought it was a great idea and encouraged us to pursue it.

We talked it over with Shannon, who very enthusiastic. But we advised him to first think about it – go and discuss it with his wife and legal representatives and come back with an answer. He came back with the same enthusiasm he'd left us with.

Then we thought of another idea to reward him even more.

This involved buying another property and separating the business completely.

Our existing premises were leased and we were really starting to outgrow them. Eventually the nursery would need to be moved to new premises and we began to look for a place we could purchase.

So we gave Shannon an opportunity to be financially involved by offering him a stake in the new property. It was the deal of a lifetime! For in exchange for 40% of the deposit, he would own 40% of the property. The repayments were all covered by the business. So in effect, for an investment of 8%, he would end up with 40% of the total lot. On a million-dollar property, that would be a capital gain of $320,000 – all paid for by the business!

We offered Shannon a generous wage, structured with huge bonuses as performance incentives. So with part ownership in the property and big bonus incentives, a guy with Shannon's capabilities was sure to be successful.

All that remained was to find the right property.

Shannon went out eagerly looking for a week or so and found the perfect place. Twenty acres in a convenient location, close enough to the existing business to be practical. The property included a large office – formerly a church administration building – and a three-bedroom house. The price tag was also impressive, but we could afford it on the back of our recent financial success.

Unfortunately Shannon struggled to come up with his share of the deposit. Despite his professional business acumen and all those years in management, he had apparently not done well financially.

This probably should have sounded alarm bells for us, but we were a long way down the road with our dream of this huge landscaping business and Shannon was an integral part of it.

Shannon was ultimately able to take out a second mortgage on his house to raise the deposit and we proceeded. We also purchased a truck, two utes, a bobcat and a backhoe, resulting in a large investment we had to get a return on. Still, we were confident Shannon would deliver.

He'd really landed the deal of a lifetime – with a relatively small investment he'd landed a major share in a substantial investment property. He would take home a significant income, regardless of performance and if he performed, he would have a very lucrative package.

This was far from a speculative venture too. We'd already proven the viability of the landscaping business with that first big contract and I was working on others. We had enormous potential for growth.

Shannon seemed appreciative and settled into his new role easily. He was a likeable guy and he got on well with his people. Perhaps if we'd been watching him more closely, we would have noticed things were a little too cosy! Of course, Shannon genuinely believed he was a good manager and his team were performing well because they liked him and liked their jobs.

All looked well. Unfortunately, it would be a very short honeymoon period and reality would soon hit us like a freight train and speed us toward the moment of impact.

LESSONS

Partnerships are very risky ventures with so many things that can go wrong. Differing views and expectations can easily like lead to unresolvable disputes. They are a lot like marriages – it is important to be clear about boundaries and expectations from the start, or one partner is bound to be disappointed as time goes on. That disappointment can lead to conflict and ultimately the end of the partnership.

Here are some of the main challenges with partnerships:

1. First and foremost, commitment levels of partners must be clearly defined. In a partnership that is an equal split, unless

both partners are fully committed and willing to put everything in the business, it is bound to lead to conflict. Partners should be open and honest about their goals with the business and what they are willing to commit to achieve those goals.

These levels of commitment could change from year to year, but for the sake of the long-term health of the business, partners should always be open and honest about it.

2. Equity in the business can be a major hurdle, as it is not always possible to do a 50/50 split with everything. If one partner provides the capital and the other brings expertise or contacts, it can be difficult to determine the partnership split in a way that satisfies both parties. There are no hard and fast rules about how expertise or contacts can be valued and if the non-financial partner falls short on the other's expectations, there can be some real conflict that will ultimately destroy the business.

   There is also the problem, with the non-financial partner being overly careless with the money – as they did not have to work for it and save it. It's the age old problem of 'other people's money'. So expectations and the financial split must be properly addressed when the partnership is formed, if the business is to survive long term.

3. Just as in equity, there can also be disparities in skills and roles of each partner. Partners usually don't have equal skill levels, as it's rare for the founding partner to find someone with exactly the skill level required for the business.

   While in some cases, partners can be skilled in different areas which are complementary, they rarely play an equal role in the success of the business.

This disparity in skills can be overcome when the under-skilled partner is willing to invest some long hours and develop their knowledge and skills so they can play a more important role in the company.

4. Different management styles can be a real headache to manage with one partner being too lax and the other too authoritarian – conflict can occur with the way the other manages the business and blame them for problems that occur. However, these different styles can sometimes be complementary and when partners recognise this, it can benefit the business with one partner keeping things on track, ensuring deadlines are met and rules are adhered to, while the other keeps employees feeling appreciated and engaged.

   Two partners with the same management style can be just as problematic, particularly when both are authoritarian, used to getting their way with everything, or both are introverted people who don't like managing staff and telling others what to do.

5. The personal habits of partners can cause major problems. How they deal with stress and if this leads to substance abuse, which then impedes their performance? Partners must work closely together, sometimes for long hours and the line between their personal and business lives can be blurred.

   It's important in a partnership that both partners are willing to cut each other a bit of slack and try and respect the other's lifestyle choices or traits. There needs to be a lot of give and take and both partners must do whatever they can to try and avoid annoying each other.

6. It's important to set boundaries right from the start. Often partners are members of the same family or friends and disagreements can spill over into their personal lives and

create more stress than they would if the partnership was purely business.

This can then compromise both their professional and personal relationships. Clear boundaries must be set right at the start of the partnership and adhered to, so that business problems are kept out of personal relationships as much as possible.

With our own partnership, something we did not do well, was clearly define expectations. We also didn't know enough about our partner's financial health and personal habits. Some simple background checks would have alerted us to something in his past that we would have found very disturbing. We'd basically trusted this guy on face value and he was very convincing in person. We'd also created a partnership deal that was very unbalanced – we were taking most of the risk, without having much control of the results. Shannon got paid his salary regardless of what happened.

The fact that our business coach had not alerted us of these problems was a good indication that we were now well and truly out of his area of expertise. We'd outgrown him. This is vital to know when you engage a business coach. Real-life experience is worth a million times more than a textbook education.

A coach without real business experience may be able to help with simple business advice but for anything beyond that, real-life experience is essential. There are just so many things that can go wrong. A good business coach would have stopped us getting into this arrangement with Shannon. They would have immediately picked up the potential problems, saving us from the catastrophe that was about to engulf us.

They would have protected us from ourselves and kept our business decisions commercial rather than emotional. We genuinely wanted to share the opportunity for success, but retrospectively this just meant we were locked into a relationship that would be very difficult to exit from.

My Notes / Thoughts

CHAPTER 17

The Classic Conman

CHAPTER 17

The Classic Conman

The best way to describe Bruce was a 'classic conman'. He could look right at you with those innocent baby blue eyes and convince you of anything. The kind of guy who could sell ice in Antarctica. Shannon stated: "I don't think we can really move the business forward the way we want to without him."

"Why is this guy so critical to our business?" Robert asked. "He's so well connected," Shannon replied. He was, he had contacts in all the top building firms in Melbourne. He knew the decision makers, the guys who would hire the landscapers. The people we needed to impress of we were going to break into that new market. And it was a huge market. Hospitals, schools, shopping centres, the holy grail of landscaping.

He'd worked for a competitor doing exactly that – and now he was available and willing to take us to a dominant position in the marketplace.

Robert trusted Shannon's judgement and agreed to go ahead. After all, we could afford it. We had a good landscaping contract with a local developer and I was working on a couple more.

Having someone with good contacts in the construction market would allow us to break into that market and become a major player in the industry.

In retrospect, on a personal level, Bruce was morally and ethically bankrupt. He treated staff with disdain, with the exception of one of the girls he had an affair with. Once the affair was over, he treated her with even more contempt than the others.

On a professional level, he continually gave us misleading information about projects and how much we'd make from them.

One thing we hadn't taken into account when we started was that major construction sites are union sites and contractors like us wishing to work on them had to have things like enterprise bargaining agreements in place with staff. It added another level of compliance, with more administration overheads.

We'd already been through that process to qualify for the local government authority tenders, but we had to take it a step further for the union sites, which of course cost time and money and meant that our quote on the jobs would have to be higher.

Bruce's contacts in construction turned out to be far less warm than he'd intimated. I doubt he really had any close friends at all, as the warmth he could turn on like a gushing fire hose, quickly faded when he didn't want anything from you. But nonetheless, he was able to leverage and manipulate them enough to win some major contracts.

Robert made sure he was involved in the first tender and helped Bruce cost it. Bruce baulked a little at the price, but proceeded anyway and to his surprise we won the contract. It was probably the only one we made a profit on.

Bruce won subsequent tenders mainly on price and they were so tight, the projects would have had to be managed extremely efficiently to break even.

Unfortunately, we later found out that Bruce had a history of undercutting competitors to win projects.

While working for a competitor previously, he'd won a major project we lost on price. We wondered at the time how they could possibly do it for the amount they'd quoted. It turns out they couldn't. The business went into liquidation.

Just a small detail Bruce had forgotten to mention in the interview.

Hiring the classic conman had been one huge mistake, which accelerated us toward the moment of impact!

LESSONS

Through our experience hiring the classic conman, we learned the painful lesson of always completing background checks on job applicants. We'd been lucky with hiring prior to Shannon and Bruce – everybody we'd hired had been everything they claimed to be and they'd excelled in their work. So we began to trust our instincts much more than we should have and it turned out to be the main error that ultimately drove us to the moment of impact.

Background checks are not that hard to do, especially with the internet at our fingertips. You should always do a search for applicant's accounts in social media. People will generally let their hair down there and you will get a glimpse of their lifestyle and the circle of friends they mix with. You'll get a feel for the amount of time they spend playing and even a hint of drug use.

One of our clients ran a dummy Facebook account, so he could 'friend' finalists for key positions and see information they're hiding from public view.

Another extremely important thing to check on applicants for key positions is if they've been bankrupt in the past. This can be done with a simple search through the relevant authority's website.

A prior bankruptcy may not necessarily disqualify that applicant for the job, but it helps paint a picture of their past and gives you a much better feel for their capabilities.

Somebody who has been bankrupt in the past and has again built up a high level of debt obviously can't manage their money and shouldn't manage any of yours.

Above all, having a wealth of information on your applicant when you interview them, will give you a good indication about how honest they are. Honesty is the most important quality required of any employee who has any level of responsibility within your organization.

My Notes / Thoughts

CHAPTER 18

The Happy Puppy

CHAPTER 18

The Happy Puppy

Shannon was a likeable guy. He was the happy puppy, lapping up affection, always wanting to please his workmates and his bosses. His seeming good relationships with staff were just Shannon craving affection and approval, not as he thought, practical rapport building.

He became known among staff as the 'soft touch', the guy who'd never confront you about anything. Nobody was ever fired or even reprimanded for anything in Shannon's team. And if you looked closely, he should have been doing a lot of firing and reprimanding.

It became evident later that Shannon was not good at managing money. He bought his teams approval by purchasing new vehicles and equipment when they asked. He knew he would always have to justify the need for the equipment to Robert and often he would sign a guarantee as a Director just to ensure the orders got through quickly.

Perhaps he bought his wife's approval too, because he couldn't even service his loan for the deposit on the property we'd bought together. After one month payment, he complained to Robert, who reluctantly gave him a pay rise so he could cover the loan.

Because of the lack of discipline he instilled in his team, employee fraud was rife. We came to realize this when our overtime bills and fuel bills went through the roof and even though staff apparently worked long hours, subcontractors still had to be hired in to finish jobs.

Work utes and equipment were obviously being used for people's personal jobs and possibly other contacts. Staff were either loafing around during regular work hours and doing work in overtime periods, or doing work for other people as well as us.

We had no way of knowing – we'd entrusted it all to Shannon and he was doing his best to be everybody's friend, including ours. When we got progress reports, they were exactly what we wanted to hear. "It's all going well; we're really going to make some money this month." When pressed about the high overtime bills, he would just say they were trying to get the job finished on time and there were no other expenses to come out anyway.

The following month, we'd be slammed with a whole bunch of overdue sub contractors' bills for the same project, taking it well and truly into the red. When confronted, Shannon always had a good reason and the additional expenses and predictions for the following month got better and better.

Our patient, caring bookkeeper loathed him. She could see things were going astray, but her sense of respect kept her from confronting him or complaining about him. We perhaps should have asked her about the problems. We certainly should have seen the warning signs way before the moment of impact!

When Robert called Shannon's wife, after the moment of impact, she blurted out "Shannon has already been bankrupt once before in his own business!" If only we'd known… this was important information!

We took full responsibility for this oversight that cost us millions of dollars, but you don't have to. Always ask the hard questions, and if necessary record the interview so you have a record of what was said. Never, ever, accept anyone's word for anything.

LESSONS

Shannon's management style taught us a lesson in managing people, particularly high 'I' personality types in management positions. These people really need someone with a 'C' personality to work with them closely and make sure they stay on track.

The 'I' type can easily get carried away with friendship and their need for approval and forget the day-to-day things that keep the business running. Like monitoring the time spent on the different tasks that make up a project.

They also don't particularly like conflict and an amount of confrontation and conflict was needed to stop employees slacking off and claiming huge amounts of overtime.

Worst of all was Shannon's habit of trying to appease us by telling us what we wanted to hear, rather than being honest about the situation. He was just basically postponing that potential conflict and in doing so, made it extremely difficult to keep our finger on the pulse.

The accounting software we started with was not adequate when the business grew. This was quickly realized. We had commissioned a new system, which would allow for better project reporting and product sales analysis. Unfortunately this was not finalised prior to the moment of impact.

In hindsight it may have been more advantageous to have implemented this system earlier. It would have given Robert the opportunity for more information than he was currently receiving and he could have kept expenses under control. Our rapid growth outgrew the accounting software; our systems could not keep up with the number of transactions. Doubling the business in the last year made managing it far more difficult than ever imagined. Always ensure to plan carefully so reporting is not overlooked.

My Notes / Thoughts

CHAPTER 19

The Unravelling

CHAPTER 19

The Unravelling

By itself, Bruce's underquoting was not enough to drive us to the point of impact. We could have dealt with those losses and Robert could have got involved again and landed some projects that gave us some profit.

It took the deadly combination of underquoting, mismanagement and inexperience to drive us into the ground so hard; it formed a crater that was very difficult to climb out of.

So Bruce underquoted the jobs, Shannon mismanaged them, and we did not have the experience to pick it up early enough and neither did the person who should have, our business coach, Richard.

It all started to unravel when our wages bills from landscaping began ringing alarm bells with our bookkeeper and with Robert too. It's not that their hourly rates were overly generous, they were on the high side, but we expected to pay that to attract the right people.

The overtime was the problem. It was out of control. Both Shannon and Bruce would reassure us that things were going well and we would soon see profits. Overtime was necessary they asserted, because of deadlines on the projects.

But the following month would be even worse, with a whole lot of unexpected and overdue invoices for subcontractors and materials used on the previous job for which 'unforeseen circumstances' would be blamed and now that we've overcome them, "we can really move forward and make money on this project".

Sadly, this became a pattern, with the projections becoming more elaborate each month and the actual losses larger. Shannon was very convincing with his explanations and despite the reality being very different, we trusted him. That is until the third month.

Robert sensed that we would need to inject more money into the business and had another loan pre-approved. Our credit rating was good, we'd been up-to-date with all our loan payments and our numbers were good up to the point where we moved the landscaping to its new location and trusted Shannon to manage it himself.

Basically, we'd stopped monitoring it, and the operation got completely out of control.

In that short space of time, Shannon changed the way the landscaping business was run completely. He appeared to have focused on being everybody's best friend at the expense of productivity. Without expectations and without consequences, staff appeared to have pushed the boundaries as far as they could, either relaxing or doing their own personal projects during working hours and then catching up with overtime.

The overtime could have been completely fraudulent. We had no way of knowing.

By the time Robert pulled it up, it was too late. We didn't realize the extent of the damage. The loan Robert organized would barely scratch the surface. We could not trade out of it.

The importance of experience for a business coach

Richard didn't have any personal business experience, nor did he have experience coaching clients as large as we'd become. We had outgrown him! He referred two of his construction clients to us, they placed orders of plants at the nursery and then both disappeared!

They had gone broke. We didn't get our money and our confidence in Richard completely disappeared at that point.

While searching for business seminars, Robert found a coach and speaker he could really identify with. The tough approach and 'No BS' message really resonated with him. We joined with that organization and a senior coach came out, went over our operation and sat down with the bookkeeper. He confirmed all our worst fears. Our landscaping operation was completely out of control. We needed to take immediate action.

Unfortunately, it was a case of too little, too late!

Other people's money

On reflection, one of the main problems we had with Shannon is that he had no financial stake in the business itself. If we lost money on a project, it had no bearing on his ability to put food on the table. Although Shannon would have loved the bonuses – they were very generous, he was obviously comfortable with the salary he was taking home, particularly after Robert increased it so he could cover his payments on the deposit for the land.

The problem was that it was just other people's money. He obviously thought we had much more cash than we did and presumed we could cover some large short-term losses.

He did not feel any financial pain, so he wasn't all that worried about the situation.

Worst of all, none of those projects should have lost money. Even though they were underquoted, had they been properly managed, we could have at least broken even on them and even made a small profit. Instead, our losses were over a million dollars.

LESSONS

It is essential to have control over your business and be able to monitor it closely, even when it is systematized and you have managers running it. A system to allow for constant monitoring of clearly defined KPIs (key performance indicators) is essential. These KPIs will vary from business to business and any reputable accountant should be able to identify the numbers relative to your particular business. When initially implemented you will need to review to ensure the information is appropriate for you to know the health of your business at a glance. The correct implementation will allow you to see when things are moving off track and allow time to correct them and get the business operating efficiently.

In our case, our landscaping manager should have been using appropriate project management software to record hours logged against each task associated with the project, and compared to the budgeted hours for each task. As each task should have been listed and quoted, this would have given us a clear indication of where we stood as the project commenced and given us an early warning signal, so we could have jumped in and brought it back under control. At the time we were trialling an accounting program that could measure these expenses but only once invoices and time sheets were logged rather than in real time. Such a system would have made it much easier to prevent misleading reporting by Shannon, our general manager of landscaping.

This has become much easier in the last few years with the move to Software as a Service (SaaS) systems, which is cloud-based software and can easily be used on mobile devices such as smartphones and tablets. The cloud is a network of computers sharing disk space and load, which protect you against hardware failure. It is also better protected against hacking or disasters than computers in your office. Initially there may be resistance to the new technology from employees and managers, but it will be worth the fight to implement.

There are good SaaS based project management applications to suit most businesses and they generally integrate with your accounting software, making it easy to keep track of your KPIs.

As business coaches who learned this lesson through bitter experience, one of the first things we do with a new business is look at their systems and reporting. How are they keeping track of their operations?

Getting this right is getting the keys to your freedom. Only when you can go online, look at your KPIs and know exactly how your business is doing at any time, can you take long holidays or reduce your working days to two per week.

It's one thing putting in systems and training staff in them. It's quite another to be able to properly monitor them. But it is essential. When you have your finger on the pulse and your employees know you're watching, they are much more likely to be diligent in their work. Employee fraud goes down and productivity goes up. As a sideline we would also recommend GPS tracking devices on all vehicles. If you can't measure it, you can't control it. If staff members have use of a vehicle for work purposes then that is what the vehicle should be used for.

And in the event things go wrong, you can quickly jump in and get everything back on track, before any real damage is done and before you lose any real money.

I can confidently say that if we'd been using a good online reporting system, that enabled us to keep track of our KPIs, our business never would have failed.

My Notes / Thoughts

CHAPTER 20

The Moment of Impact

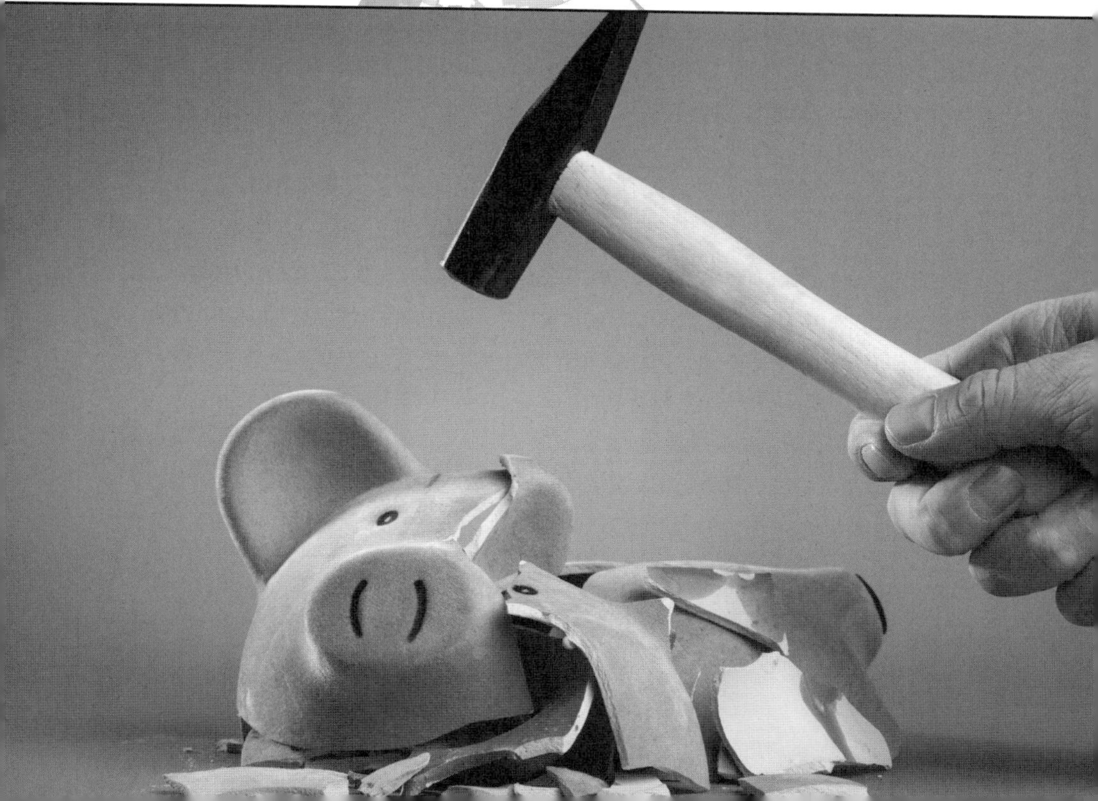

CHAPTER 20

The Moment of Impact

"Why did you set it up like that?" The accountant sat stony-faced, unflinching. He rolled his eyes as if it were an unreasonable question. "It works well, when the business is going good," he said. Then added: "It's just not a good structure if you fail."

We were shocked, horrified and furious. Why hadn't they bothered to explain this to us? They had come highly recommended by Robert's colleagues in banking, so we trusted them completely and paid them a small fortune over the years…

But the businesses had been structured in a way that left us completely vulnerable to creditors. When we reached the moment of impact, we thought that perhaps we could save the nursery and just liquidate the landscaping, which had accumulated all the losses and was dragging down the other business which had always been profitable.

"Not possible," we were told – the businesses were cross-collateralised, meaning that they were effectively one business.

Robert had already determined that the landscaping business could not trade out of its current financial situation and the accountant agreed. Bruce, the business development manager who'd been doing all the quoting, had dropped right off in the last couple of months as the business was unravelling, so there were few new projects coming through, but there were a number of projects in various stages of completion.

The nursery business through all the traumas had consistently been profitable and could have traded on if it had been a separate unconnected business. During the time the landscaping business had been making a loss the nursery had been supporting it and consequently it was short of cash and struggling to pay its bills. In a bid to keep the promised landscaping profits we had sacrificed the 'cash cow' and had no way to reverse the situation. In retrospect we should have not poured hundreds of thousands of dollars into that business, we should have let it live or die by its own efforts. That is easy to say in retrospect while at the time is like choosing which of your two children to let die, like in the movie *Sophie's Choice*. Then perhaps we could at least save the house... After all, the loans were paid, so there was no claim on it. "Not necessarily," they said. "As a director, the creditors could come after you." Why then had I been listed as director? Why not just a shareholder? This was Accounting 101!

Feeling angry and cheated, we resigned ourselves to our fate. The accountant recommended that we appoint a liquidator, recommending someone that they had used previously, referring to them as a 'friendly liquidator' which seemed like an oxymoron. Our accountant then handed us on to another partner, whom we had never met before, who specialised in this sort of thing and he liaised with the liquidator and advised us what to do. As a final irony the accountant took our last $80,000 to pay themselves and the liquidator and left the business totally broke. It still seems really odd that we had to pay to lose everything!

If you've never been through liquidation, the best way I could describe it is like taking your prize cow that has been your sole source of income and watching a pack of wolves devour it, while the creditors look on from the sidelines, like hawks – picking up whatever scraps they can get.

It was an incredibly stressful time and there was nothing but uncertainty, regret and soul searching. What should we have done differently, it only seemed a couple of days ago when we were on top of the world and extremely successful. Did we really manage to stuff it up so completely?

Generally speaking a business doesn't fail because one thing goes wrong (except when you have one major client). It takes a number of things to happen. In our case the following reasons contributed to the final collapse.

1. Poor recruitment of senior management.
2. Ineffective reporting procedures.
3. A belief that we had overcome an initial downturn which we survived and then had grown the business every year by 20–60% and that we were almost bullet proof.
4. Choosing not to confront senior staff about their performance in a manner that had consequences attached to it, rather than being concerned that if they left we would be unable to manage and complete the projects we had on the go at the time.
5. Buying a business asset with an employee. This act of generosity was probably the dumbest thing we did and effectively locked us into the relationship. We had wanted to incentivise and reward what we considered a key employee; instead we created a rod for our own backs, and practically made it almost impossible to fire him.
6. Giving people the benefit of the doubt and trusting that they knew what they were doing in a business that was doing major and complex projects.
7. Poor financial advice and structuring by the accountant.
8. Growth at any cost in the last year we grew almost 100%. However, this would not have been a problem if we would have been profitable.

As Robert had signed guarantees for creditors of the landscaping business he had no choice but to go bankrupt, while Lorraine would stay out of it – and by some miracle we could keep the house. This was never really a reality as despite two mortgages on the property there was still some equity that they could be realized even though by the time it was sold there was little left to pay the creditors. It is a part of the process and we paid the price for bad advice. Shannon also suffered the same fate as he had signed guarantees to the same creditors and they forced him into bankruptcy for a second time. We could never understand why he would accept such a financial burden as he had no equity in the business and essentially nothing to gain from it. Maybe it just highlights inexperience and business naivety – and to think we let him manage a $6 million business. More fool us. So we'd completely underestimated the moment of impact. It at first seemed we could control the damage, but it quickly spread like a raging bushfire, consuming everything.

LESSONS

It is still incredible to believe that a professional accounting firm could be so negligent in their advice. We must reiterate it's vitally important to structure a company properly right from the start. It is extremely difficult to change once you start operating, so you need the best possible advice at this point. That old saying, "Hope for the best, but plan for the worst" is something you should keep in the back of your mind when structuring your company.

Don't fall into the trap of trusting your accountant completely, because they came highly recommended, like we did. Ask them to explain their proposed structure. Then test it with different worst-case scenarios. Ask questions like an investigative journalist. Make sure your personal assets are protected, regardless of what happens in the business.

Nobody ever goes into business with the belief that they will fail, but there are a myriad of things that can go wrong and you need to protect your family in the event that they do.

Get a second opinion from a lawyer if you're unsure, or you don't like their explanation. The money you spend at the start will pay you dividends further down the line. You're getting the foundation of your business set up properly and that's not something you want to skimp on.

As well as looking at 'doomsday scenarios', you should look at what will happen if things go better than planned. Will the company structure you're setting up allow for expansion? What will you do if you start a complementary service like we did? Can you keep it as a separate entity under your current structure and not cross-collateralise it so it can be one day sold as a separate entity?

If you sign a guarantee on behalf of the business expect that at some stage that may become a real liability and you will be liable for payment. Robert had no assets in his name and so there was little reason to make him bankrupt other than to make a point. From a practical point of view no financial advantage was gained.

Finally, you need to ask how the proposed business structure affects your rate of taxation. What about other taxes like capital gains? In some cases, you may be better putting it under a Trust rather than a company.

This will all impact on your income and your lifestyle at some stage.

My Notes / Thoughts

CHAPTER 21

Goodbye Old Friend

CHAPTER 21

Goodbye Old Friend

Nothing we'd experienced, right through our business challenges, could have prepared us for this. Rejection from prospects was hard to take, but nothing was as emotionally crushing as good friends and family abandoning us.

Robert and I had always enjoyed a very active social life and we had many good friends whom we'd known for decades. Friends were important to us and even though we worked hard, we always found time for them. We supported each other through challenges and shared celebrations.

We were particularly close to one couple, Simon and Kate, who we had much in common with. We travelled overseas together during our vacations, celebrate birthdays together and just basically enjoyed each other's company.

When Simon was diagnosed with cancer, we were there to support him in any way we could. It was a difficult couple of years as he struggled with the horrible effects of chemotherapy and the emotional roller coaster that goes with death hanging over your head. The possibility of being snatched away from friends and family…

But he pulled through and we laughed together and celebrated his survival.

So as our world collapsed around us, we naturally reached out to Kate and Simon, but they weren't around. Thankfully other friends were, so we weren't totally alone. But we kept wondering about Kate and Simon. Why weren't they returning calls or texts?

We knew what to expect, but really dreaded it. Their crushing text finally came one morning: "We don't like what is happening and we don't really want to associate with you anymore."

As shocked as we were at the desertion of old friends the way some of our family members treated us was even worse. They say that blood is thicker than water and that families stick together. Well we have to tell you that this is not always the case. Some of our close family took great delight in spreading news of our failure as far and wide as possible, revelling in our misery. Maybe deep-seated resentment at our previous success or just the chance to stick the boot in, who knows, but it is not what you expect.

But other friends were solid gold. They shone through the gloom like a lighthouse beacon. They were there for us when we needed them. We didn't need to ask for financial help, nor did we need a shoulder to cry on… We just needed friends to treat us like they always had, to give us something constant during these turbulent times – to give us a sense of normality.

We were also determined to keep life as consistent as possible for our own family and especially our son. The liquidation process was incredibly stressful and it wasn't hard to see why a lot of marriages fall apart as a result of it. But we held on together, keeping things as normal as we could in the home. We kept our son in the same school, despite the fees being incredibly hard to raise through the liquidation process and Robert's bankruptcy. And it was those special friends who stuck with us, that really enabled us to do that. Just by standing with us and saying: "I don't care what has happened; we're still friends, just the same as ever."

When the chips are down you find who your real friends are. Fair weather friends will never really be there for you if it doesn't suit them, so in many regards we are better off without them.

LESSONS

There is an old saying, "You don't really know who your friends are, until you go through a crisis" and we found out just how true this is. A crisis always brings out the best and worst in people. Just look at any natural disaster – there are people who put everything on hold and go out to help others, and there are those who take advantage of the situation for personal gain.

We truly hope you never have to experience what we went through and the lessons in this book should help prevent that, but if you do, remember the importance of keeping your family and your personal life together.

By doing that, people respected us and some friends decided to stick by us, despite many others turning their back on us.

You can emerge from a crisis like this stronger and wiser – ready to start again. We certainly did. But had we not stayed strong together, that would not have been the case.

We avoided the temptation to blame each other, what had happened, had happened, and nothing was going to change that.

It is also essential that you take full responsibility for your mistakes. Only when you do that, do you empower yourself to change and avoid making those mistakes again.

When people blame somebody else, they keep the solution beyond their control and are doomed to experience the same problem over and over again.

The classic example of this is people saying to others, "You make me so angry". This implies that the other person is controlling their emotions and they personally are unable to prevent their anger. By blaming the other person, they effectively rob themselves of the solution and are doomed to continue escalating their anger, every time the person they blame chooses to make them that way.

When you don't learn from a lesson, life has a way of giving it to you over and over again. So if you don't like your situation, the only way to change it is to take full responsibility for where you are now – and to make the necessary changes to create a different result. Sounds easy but it took us a little while to take stock and be able to say it was our fault! Once we had done that we could move on.

My Notes / Thoughts

CHAPTER 22

The Warriors Awaken

CHAPTER 22

The Warriors Awaken

Many months before the Moment of Impact we had booked and paid for a Ten-Day Intensive Workshop in Malaysia. We had no idea what to expect but decided to go as everything had been paid for and we thought a change of scenery would be good for us. We arrived in the middle of their summer with 80% humidity and a wall of heat, with no idea what to expect.

I looked up at where we had to climb – it was high… maybe 20 metres. Beads of sweat started to run down the sides of my head onto my neck. It was 6 am, but already warm and humid. It was always steamy in this jungle.

I looked up again and I felt fear trying to grip me. It started to rise up to my chest, making my breathing tight. I pushed it down, saying "Thank you, but I don't need you now." It was something we'd been practising over and over. My chest began to ease and my body relaxed. I was in control.

I looked around at Robert and the rest of my tribe. They were smiling at me confidently. I smiled back and began climbing the flimsy ladder.

For ten gruelling days, we put ourselves through activities I never thought I would have been able to do, physically or mentally. Fear would have prevented me from even trying, but now I knew how to live with fear… how to control it.

Looking back it seems that somehow this was part of a greater plan and we were being given the basis for a new start, even though at the time we were totally unaware. The physical and mental challenges took our focus off the things we had left behind and focussed them on the possibilities that were available in the future. By being so detached from our reality, it allowed us to consider the future without constant reflection on the things that had happened to us. There were over 100 people on the same adventure from all parts of the world. We gained inspiration from the way they acted as a group, all looking out for each other, despite having never met before, but also from the amazing individual strengths shown by the most physically disadvantaged. I can still remember their persistence and outright courage in face of obstacles that were very challenging for fit people in their prime. I suppose we came to realize that all we had lost was money and if we were determined we could get it back. So we decided that is what we would do and we would find a vehicle to do so and attract it with all the fervour we could muster.

When we got back to civilisation, we would use the skills we'd learned at this training camp to embark on a whole new business adventure. The fear that normally follows failure would not even slow us down. We weren't going to ignore it, or try to kill it. Fear has a purpose. Anyone without it is abnormal and reckless. We had fear but now we understood how to keep it in check.

Back at home, all hell had broken loose, we were set to lose everything and they could take everything away from us except what was inside us. We had gained an incredible amount of knowledge, but knowledge by itself is virtually useless. It is the application of knowledge that is powerful and applying it takes the right mindset, the right attitude. That was what we went away to develop.

People who believe in the law of attraction will tell you that you attract what you focus on and not what you desire or need. By going away to that camp, we took our focus off the liquidation and bankruptcy and put it firmly on moving forward. We were looking for the next opportunity.

It came so quickly, we could hardly believe it. A colleague of a mentor who had looked over our organization and cautioned us in the final days gave us a call. He wanted to meet with us. We laughed at the thought of him trying to provide coaching – the business no longer existed.

But he had something else in mind.

"Have you thought about helping other business owners?" he asked. "You have such an incredible wealth of knowledge. You have faced almost every business challenge that it's possible to face. And you overcame all but the last one."

He suggested we were probably the most highly qualified people to become business coaches as we had actually run a business both successfully and not so successfully, but our knowledge and learnings would be invaluable to all business owners.

As you can imagine, we didn't have to think about it for too long. This is where our hearts were. We couldn't bear the thought of other business owners going through the same devastation we'd had to endure. This was the logical next step for us: to build a business by helping others become successful. We couldn't think of a more worthy mission to embark on.

We immediately made plans to complete the specialist training required and set our sights on our new adventure.

We were warriors, ready to fight and conquer again and to help others win their battles.

LESSONS

The famous sales trainer, Zig Ziglar had a saying: *"Your attitude, not your aptitude, will determine your altitude."* Nothing could be more accurate. Regardless of your skills and the opportunities placed in front of you, if you do not have the right attitude and expect the best outcome, you will not succeed.

Too often when we struggle with our business, our outlook becomes gloomy, we focus on challenges and we continue to attract more challenges. At worst, we can lose all motivation.

It's important that if we begin to fall into this trap, we take action to break the cycle and become positive and optimistic. This is often easier said than done. It's extremely hard to see any light at the end of the tunnel, when you go through tough times – in our case, a bankruptcy and liquidation.

So sometimes it takes drastic action.

Remove yourself from the situation completely, find a training and motivational camp or seminar to go to, then come back and look at your situation with fresh eyes. Where you previously saw only gloom, you will now see solutions. You will wonder why you were ever so depressed about it.

For us, it was not just the motivational training the camp provided, but also hard physical challenges that made it impossible to focus on anything but the tasks we had at hand. This was the key in overcoming the stress and being able to come back renewed and ready to start again.

Most people don't want to leave a crisis. We convince ourselves that we need to stay in the trenches, to keep fighting or it will all fall apart without us – but often, that's not the case. You may be surprised about how little of a difference you were making in your gloomy state of mind.

Get your mindset right and you will be amazed at what is possible.

My Notes / Thoughts

CHAPTER 23

Epilogue

CHAPTER 23

Epilogue

As a result of this journey both Rob and I, as two individuals, have gained a wealth of information and experience to provide to people. It gave us the ability to very quickly identify any anomalies in any business and quickly correct these.

After determining our path forward we embarked on a mission of connecting with as many people as possible to walk beside them and not only to grow their businesses, but protect them from anything that may be detrimental.

This is our passion.

About The Authors

Lorraine Brooks And Rob Duncan

Lorraine Brooks was born in Melbourne, Australia and is the founder of Strategic Business Coaching & Marketing and Strategic Coaching Academy. Rob Duncan was born in Southport, United Kingdom and is the founder of Website Designer Group and Funnel Designer Group.

Both Lorraine and Rob came from a corporate background where Lorraine was heavily involved in Information Technology, Training, and Telecommunications, whilst Rob holds a Bachelor of Business in Banking and Finance degree and was a senior manager in the Banking and Finance world.

Strategic Business Coaching & Marketing was started because Mal Emery, a highly regarded business professional and mentor, approached Lorraine and Rob after they had exited from their own business and suggested they share all the good and hard lessons they had learnt. With the experience Lorraine and Rob had in growing an $11 million dollar business there is valuable information, which could form the basis of a very powerful alliance to work closely with business owners, start-ups, and entrepreneurs, teaching them what they knew and to prevent anyone from experiencing what they had endured. After all you cannot exchange real-life experience with something which you learn or read in a text book.

When Lorraine and Rob started Strategic Business Coaching and Marketing they had extremely limited financial resources. However, they had learnt the value of consulting with the top professionals so they invested in knowledge, especially marketing and proven systems for business growth. These investments have paid handsome dividends not only for themselves, but also for their clients. Lorraine and Rob continue to invest money into their education to keep themselves at the cutting edge.

Strategic Coaching Academy was developed because Lorraine and Rob wanted to make available to every person the opportunity to gain the much needed business knowledge, which is not readily available. So they built an extensive online business coaching and marketing system allowing any business owner, no matter what a person's circumstance may be, to learn everything you need to know to build a $1 million + business.

Website Designer Group and Funnel Designer Group were also established because Lorraine and Rob were looking at the bigger picture and it allowed them to offer a total business solution.

As a consequence of Lorraine and Rob's practical experience and education they are able to consistently grow and turn businesses around in a very short period of time. Lorraine and Rob have created several multimillion dollar businesses; not only have they done this again for themselves, but also for a large number of business owners. And, if you look at the other end of the spectrum they have also taken businesses which are in absolute dire straits and who are knocking on the liquidator's door and brought them back into profit. Something, which at the time, the business owner did not in their wildest dreams think it possible.

Lorraine and Rob are today sought after business advisers and have travelled the world meeting and learning from some of the very best teachers and business leaders on the planet including Tony Robbins, Alex Mandossian, Mal Emery, Jay Abrahams, Jay Conrad Levinson, Robert Kiyosaki, Russell Brunson and Brad Sugars.

Lorraine and Rob can assure you that if you have the desire to take a leap of faith and courage to get serious about your business, it will reward you like no other opportunity presented to you. They hope you enjoyed the journey with them and when you are ready, Lorraine and Rob would love your feedback regarding their Moment of Impact and what effect the information has on your life.

Recommended Resources

Business Success Tool

Imagine what you could accomplish working one-on-one with not just one but two business advisors who have created three multimillion dollar businesses

The Strategic Business Coaching Program combines the full power of both Lorraine and Rob's knowledge in both business and marketing. Lorraine and Rob only work with 5 private clients at a time, which become part of Lorraine and Rob's inner sanctum. Every client that has followed Lorraine and Rob's coaching and mentoring to the letter has achieved from 200% – 1000% improvement in their businesses.

Along with personal coaching, the Strategic Business Coaching Program includes a complete strategic audit of your company and an action plan for dramatic turn-around implementation plus full access to our Online

E-Learning Business and Marketing Program providing full access to all business and marketing templates.

If you are serious about taking your business to the next level then applying for the Strategic Business Coaching Program could be the next step in helping you achieve your ultimate goals of business and lifestyle success.

☞ To find out if our Personal Coaching Program is right for you call

1300 366 710

or email: **enquiries@strategicbusinesscoaching.net.au**

Business Success Tool

Does Your Website Attract Clients?

Website Designer Group was created from a frustration with Website Designers who cared more about themselves than their client needs. Rob's passion is building websites that achieve the goals and objectives of his clients. A website must be functional and can achieve great things with the right SEO Marketing Strategies

Website Designer Group is a dedicated Website Design, Website Development and Lead Generation business based in Australia. All website design features are fully mobile responsive, high quality websites at affordable prices for small and medium sized businesses throughout Australia. Clients choose us because we get to know their business and we are there for the long term. The websites that our clients receive are built on the principles of creative design, complete functionality.

Rob's Business Coaching Background Is Vital In Understanding What Clients Want

Rob's background is in business coaching which allows him help our client find areas to expand their businesses by recognising opportunities and formulating strategies to capitalise on them. What he offers to his clients is personalised service and a high level of customer support both during and after the website development stage.

A Complete Service is Provided

Support is from our head office in Melbourne, Victoria and is 100% onshore. It has never been more essential for all businesses to have an online presence, as 98% of your clients/prospects will search for your business on the internet before doing business with you. If you do not have a website presence then it is highly unlikely that they will consider doing business with you. If you do have a website make sure that it is able to let the visitor know immediately what your business does and how they can contact you. There has never been a better time to become a part of the online community and establish your business online. Make sure you choose a website designer who is able to understand the needs of your business and help create your brand on-line.

"I engaged Rob to build our new business website. Their level of support has exceeded my expectations. Their level of service has been exceptional and made the whole process of building and launching it in February 2016 a seamless process. Working with them has been a pleasure and I strongly recommend their services to you."

Ross Anderson

Aquagold Consulting Pty Ltd

☞ To find out if your Website is maximizing all possible opportunities call **1300 366 710** or go to **www.websitedesignergroup.com**

Resource Directory

To help you start out on your business journey we have included some resources that may be able to assist. There is a multitude of magazines, websites and books available that have up to date information. Your education should be a never ending process.

Recommended Films

The Pursuit of Happyness, Sony Pictures

Pay It Forward, Warner Bros. Pictures

The Karate Kid, Columbia & Sony Pictures

The Secret, Rhonda Byrne

Beyond the Secret, Rhonda Byrne Rocky, United Artists

Magazines

AFR Smart Investor

Wealth Creator

My Business BRW

Australian Property Investor

Books Lorraine & Rob Recommend

The E-myth, Michael Gerber

The 7 Habits of Highly Effective People, Stephen R. Covey

The Five Dysfunctions of a Team, Patrick Lencioni

The Magic of Believing, Claude Bristol

The Secret, Rhonda Byrne

Rich Dad Poor Dad, Robert Kiyosaki

Feel the Fear and Do It Anyway, Susan Jeffers

The Law of Attraction, Esther and Jerry Hicks

Money and the Law Attraction, Esther and Jerry Hicks

Think and Grow Rich, Napoleon Hill

You Were Born Rich, Bob Proctor

The Answer, John Assaraf & Murray Smith

Having It All, John Assaraf

The Monk who Sold his Ferrari, Robin S. Sharma

Fish, Stephen C. Lundin, Ph.D., Harry Paul and John Christensen

The Saint, the Surfer and the CEO, Robin S. Sharma

The Fish that Ate the Whale, Rich Cohen

Purple Cow, Seth Godin

Good to Great, Jim Collins

Who Moved My Cheese?, Dr Spencer Johnson

The Books You Read and the People You Meet, Charlie Tremendous Jones

Influence The Psychology of Persuasion, Robert B. Cialdini

Australia's Money Secrets of the Rich, John R. Burley

Money Master the Game, Tony Robbins

Grinding It Out, Ray Kroc

The Generosity Factor, Ken Blanchard

The Richest Man In Babylon, George S. Clason

Zig Ziglar's Leadership & Success Series, ***Zig Ziglar Born To Win***, Zig Ziglar

Secrets of the Millionaire Mind, T. Harv Eker

How To Persuade People Who Don't Want To Be Persuaded, Joel Bauer

The Psychology of Selling: Increase Your Sales Faster and Easier Than You Ever Thought Possible, Brian Tracy

Quantum Warrior: The Future of the Mind, John Kehoe

Board Games

Cashflow 101, Robert Kiyosaki

Cashflow for Kids, Robert Kiyosaki

Call Up, Put Down – The Stock Market Options Game, Trading Pursuits